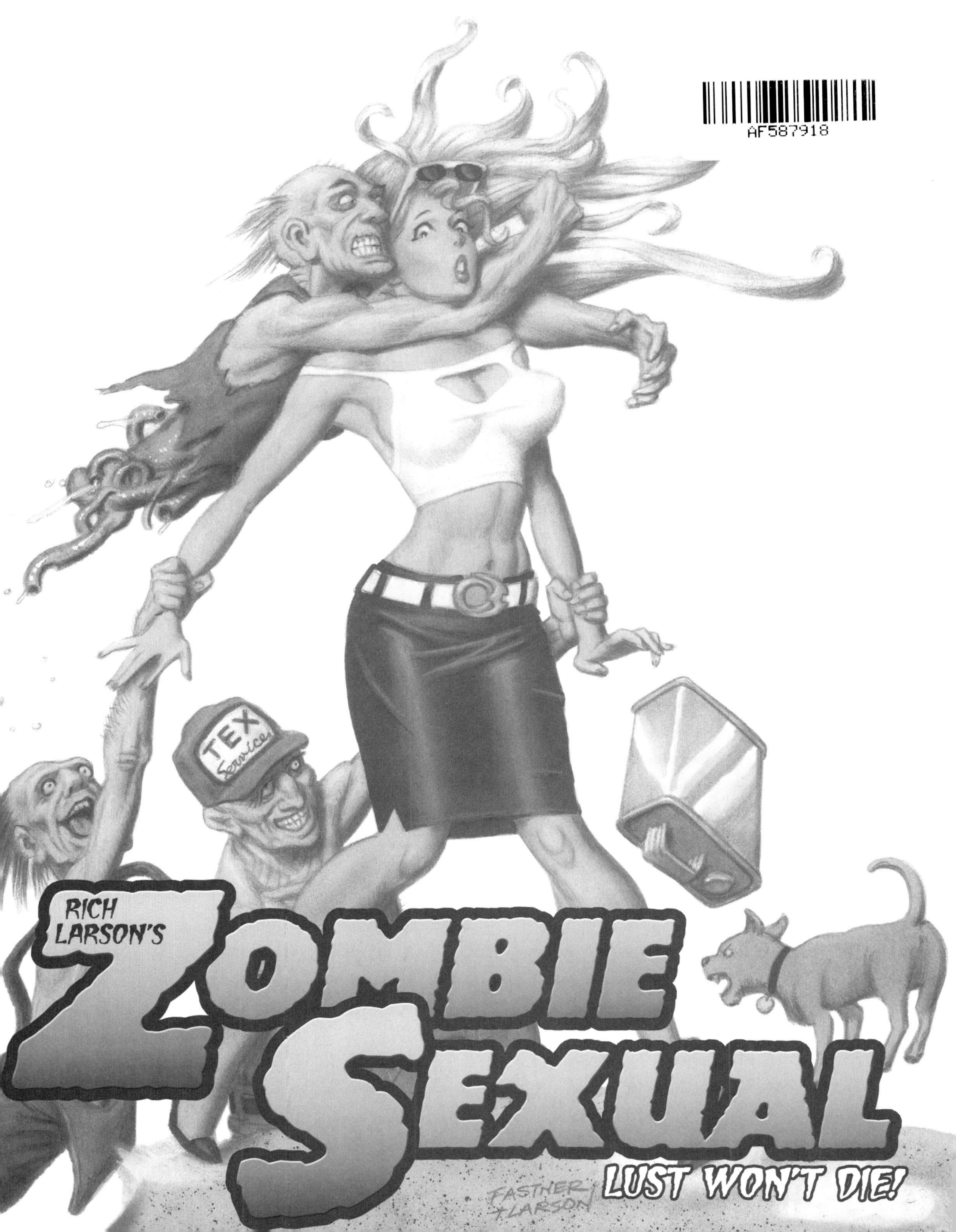
AF587918
TEX
Service
RICH LARSON'S
ZOMBIE SEXUAL
LUST WON'T DIE!
FASTNER + LARSON

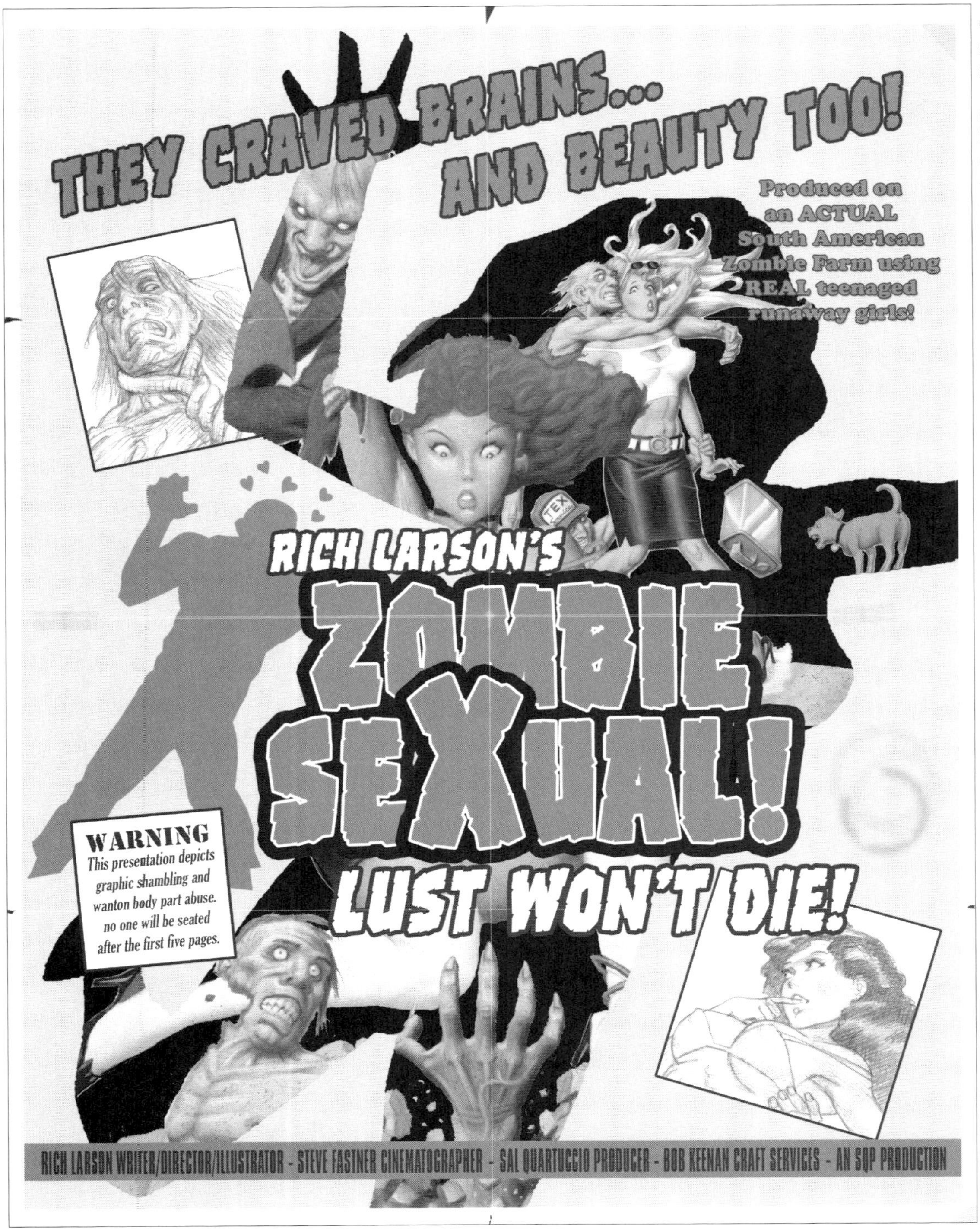

THEY CRAVED BRAINS... AND BEAUTY TOO!

Produced on an ACTUAL South American Zombie Farm using REAL teenaged runaway girls!

RICH LARSON'S

ZOMBIE SEXUAL!

LUST WON'T DIE!

WARNING
This presentation depicts graphic shambling and wanton body part abuse. no one will be seated after the first five pages.

RICH LARSON WRITER/DIRECTOR/ILLUSTRATOR - STEVE FASTNER CINEMATOGRAPHER - SAL QUARTUCCIO PRODUCER - BOB KEENAN CRAFT SERVICES - AN SQP PRODUCTION

The following is actual dialog from the 1971 film-classic **Zombie Sexual! - Lust Wont Die!**

Scene: Later that night at Señor Ricardo's House of Moist Delights, a nasty little off-the-main-road cantina. Vickie & Doreen, co-eds on vacation in South America, enter in search of a cold beer.

Doreen:
Excuse me, por favor!
Dos cervezas!

Bartender:
Si.

Vicki:
Three years of Spanish, I'm impressed!

Doreen:
Bite me, Vicki! This is the first place in 100 miles that even looks semi-civilized! What happened to Ft Lauderdale for Spring Break? Why here in the middle of el-bum-fucko South America?

Vicki:
A little adventure never hurt anyone! It's the 70's! It's time to cut loose and have some fun! We're two American girls, alone in a foreign country with plenty of money and no one watching over our every move! It's freedom, Doreen! Drink it down with your beer and quit your whining!

Doreen:
Ahhh...my beer has an eye floating in it.

Vicki:
Very funny! It's probably just a joke they play on the tourists!

Doreen:
So why does the bartender have a rotting eye socket?

Both scream in unison:
ZOMBIES! IIEEEEEE!!!!

Rich Larson's
ZOMBIE SEXUAL
Volume One

Book design by Grassy Knoll Studios.

Published by
SQP Inc.
PO Box 248 - Columbus, NJ 08022

Sal Quartuccio & Bob Keenan - Publishers

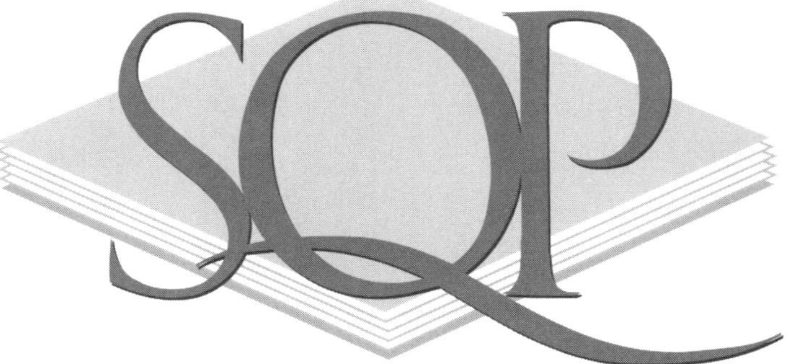

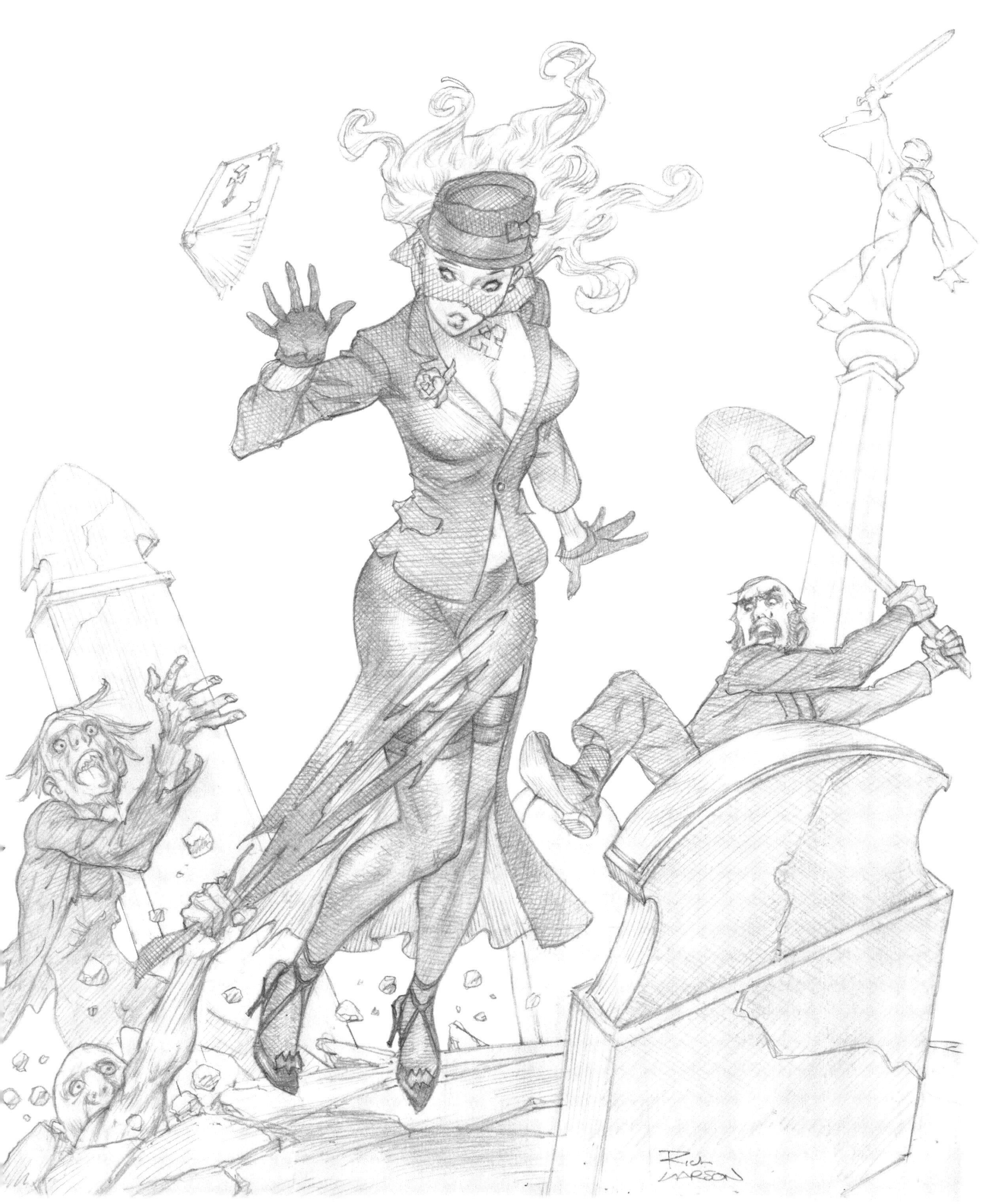

LAST RESPECTS

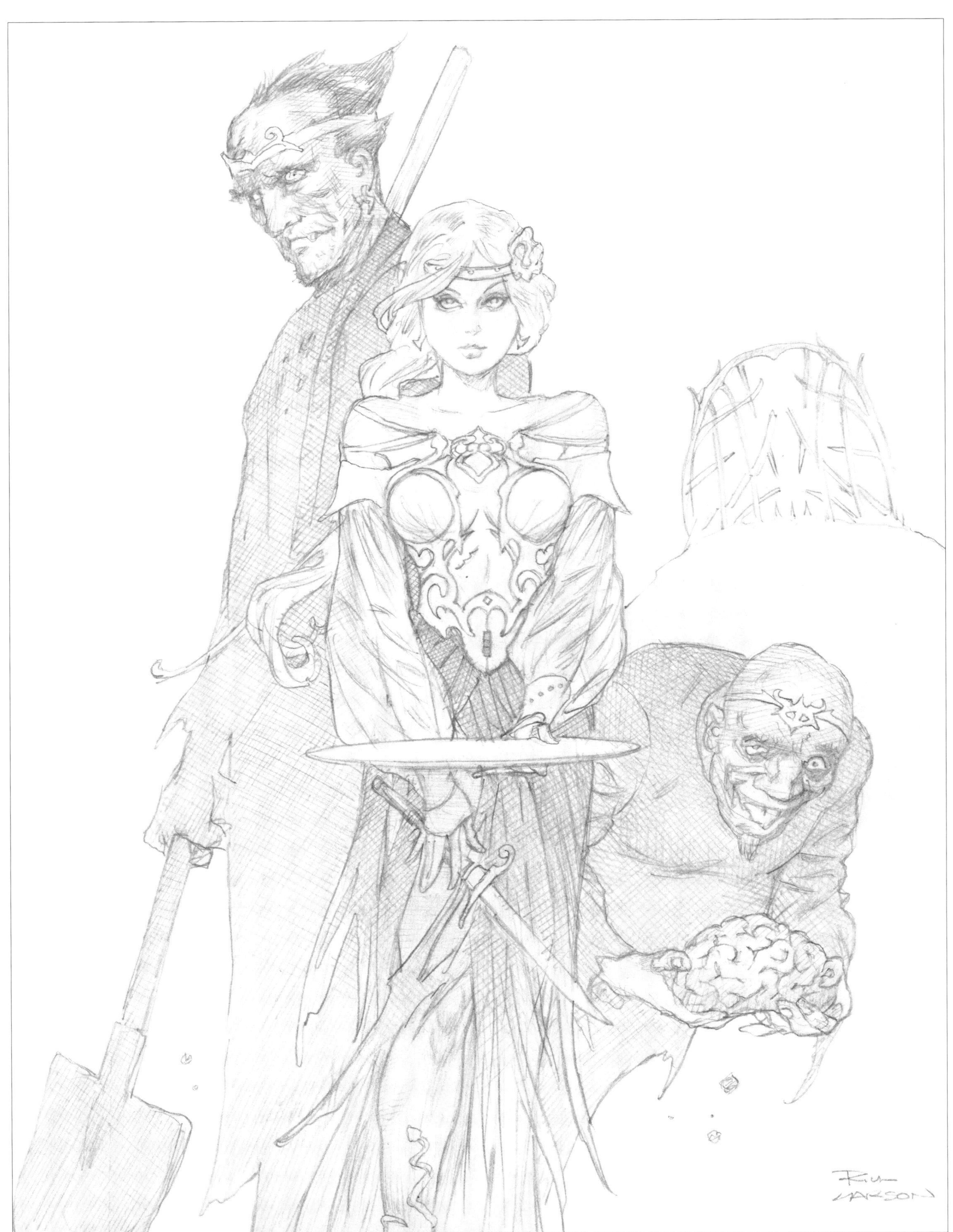

CATERERS

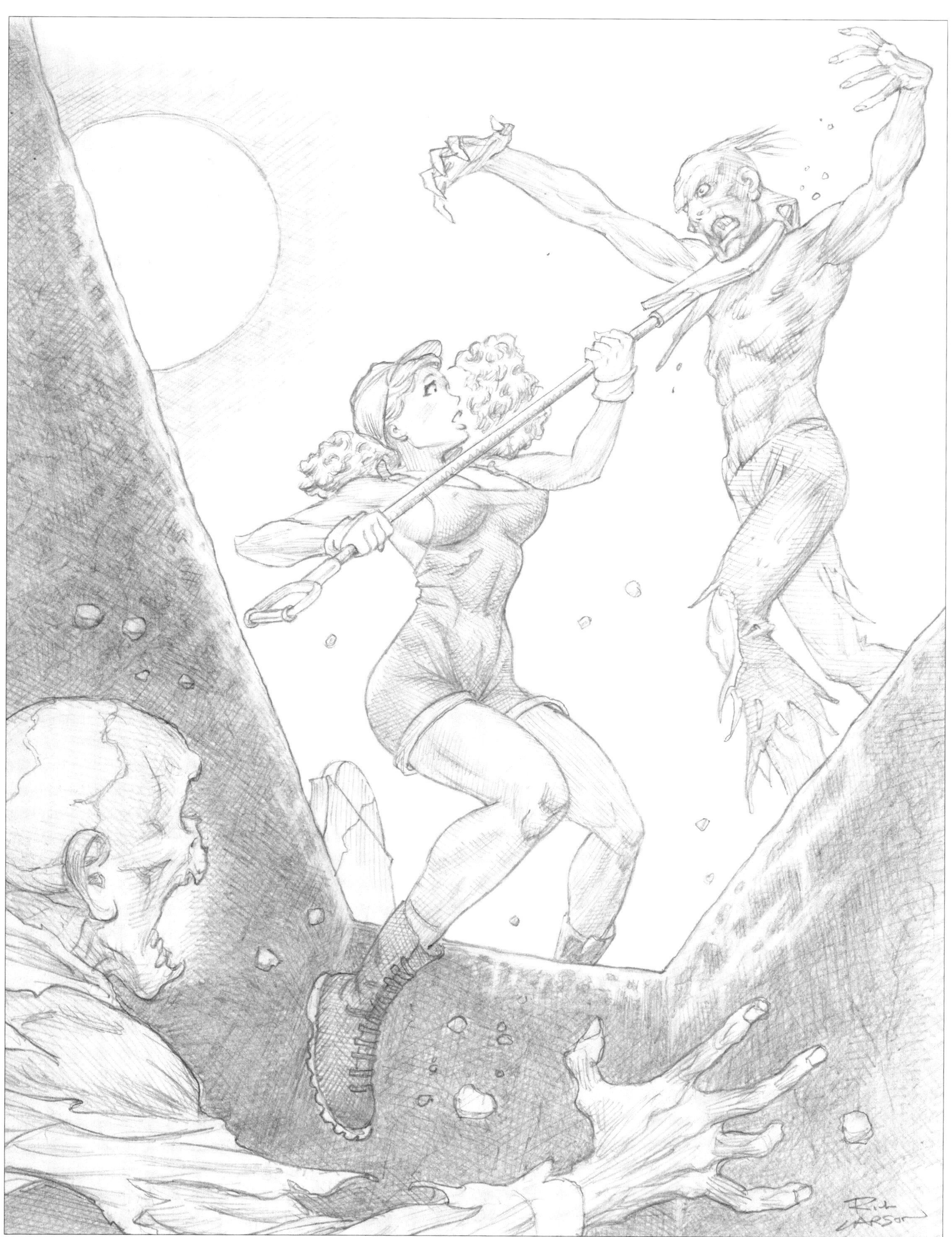

GRAVEYARD SHIFT

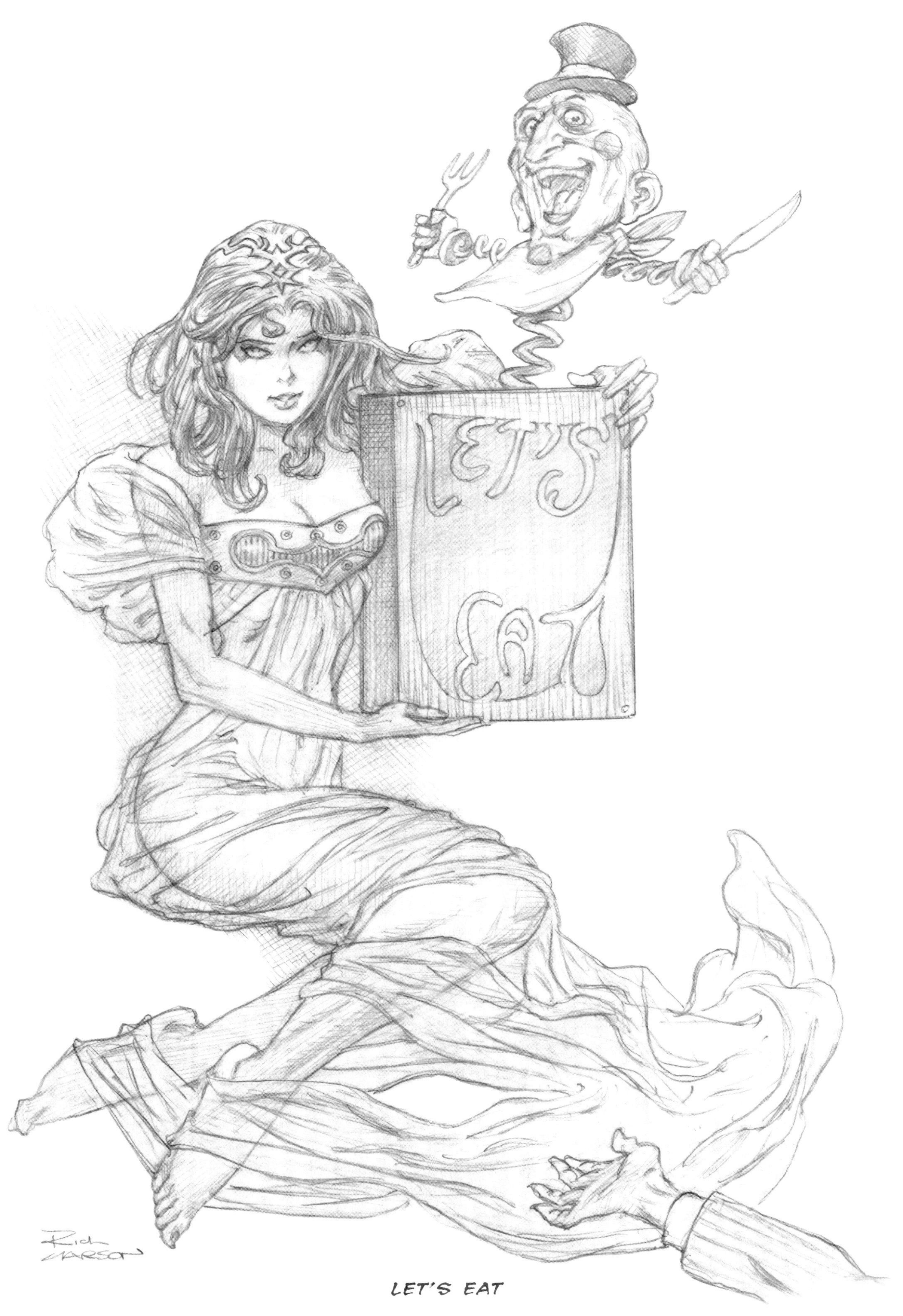

LET'S EAT

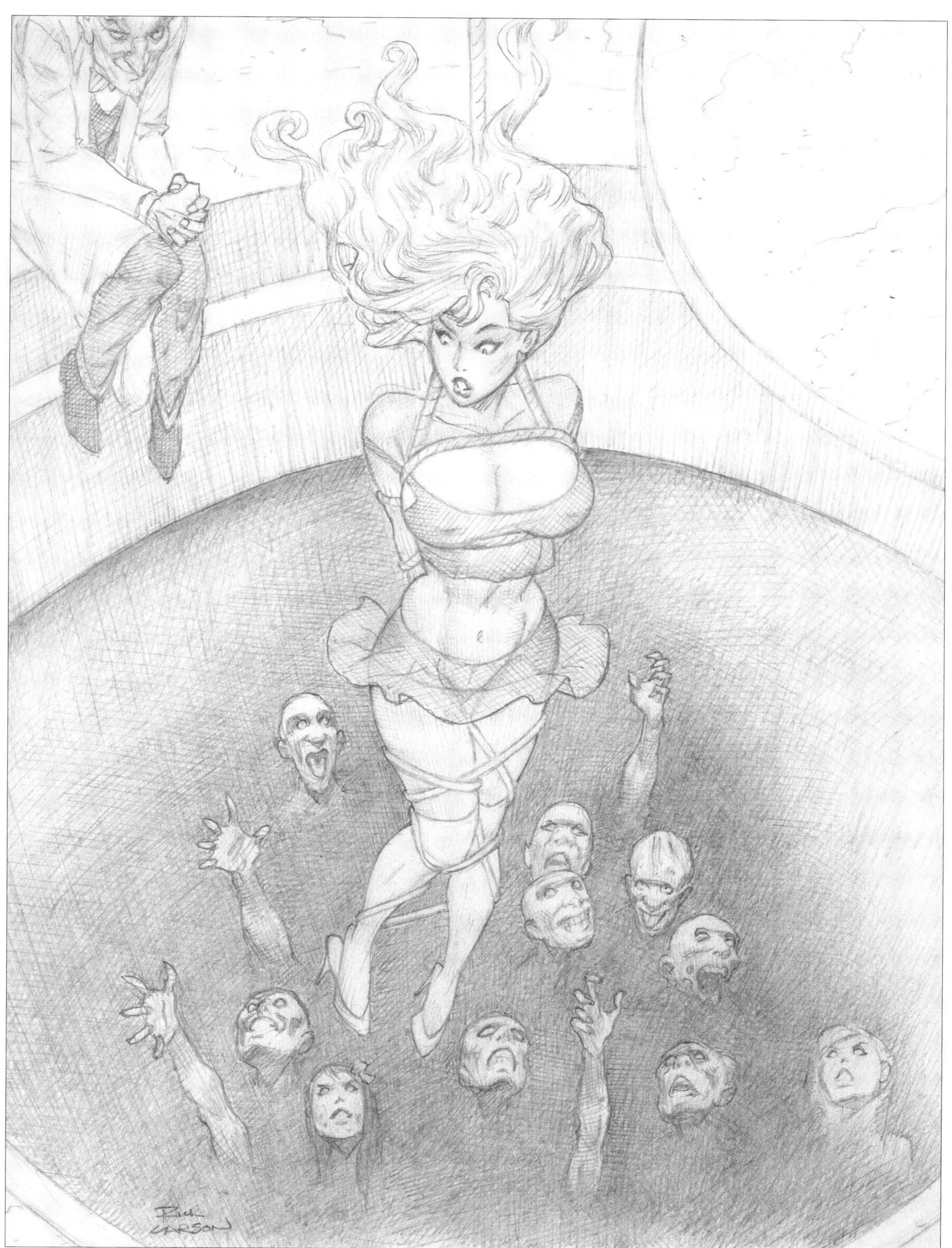

INTO THE TANK

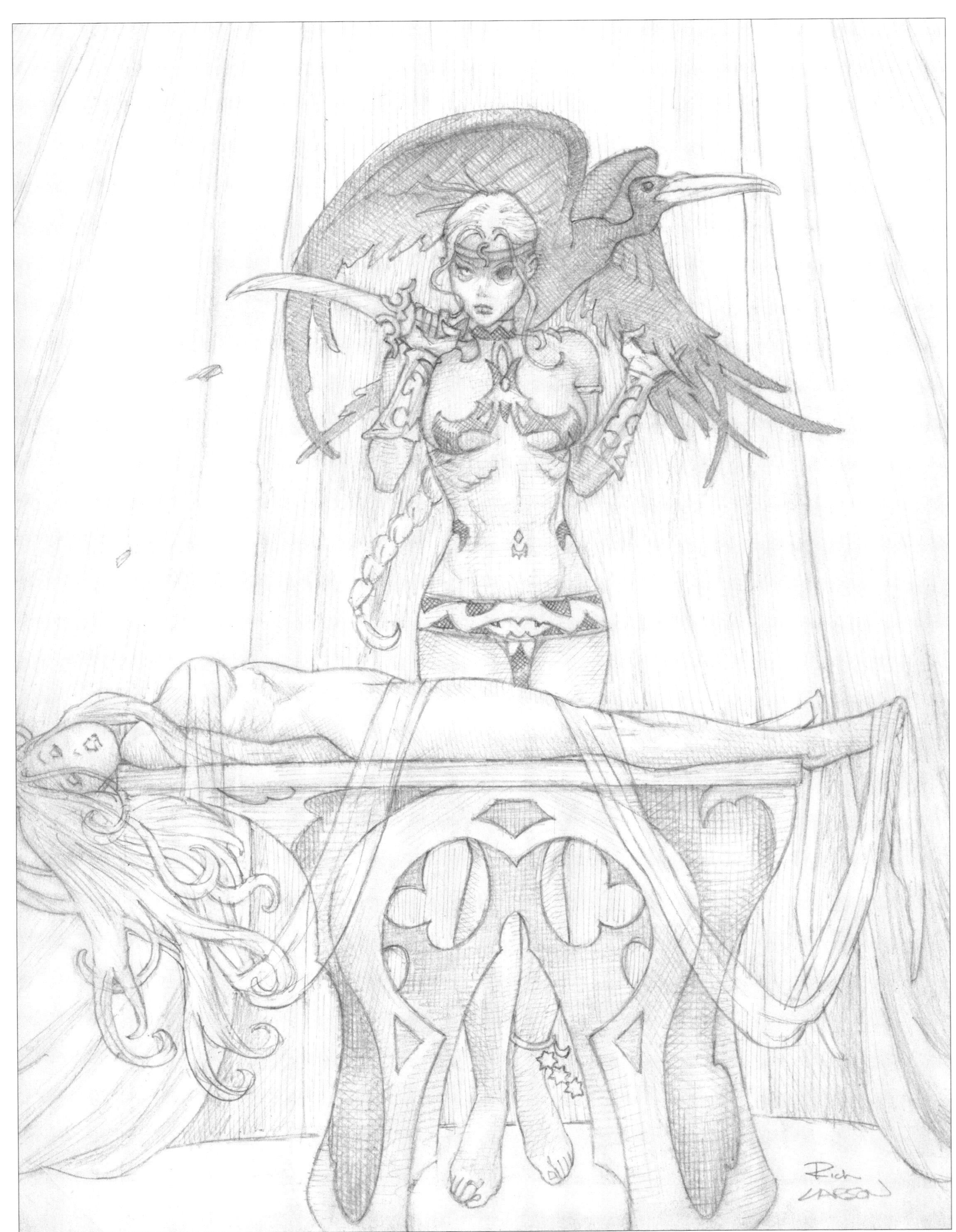

NEWBLOOD

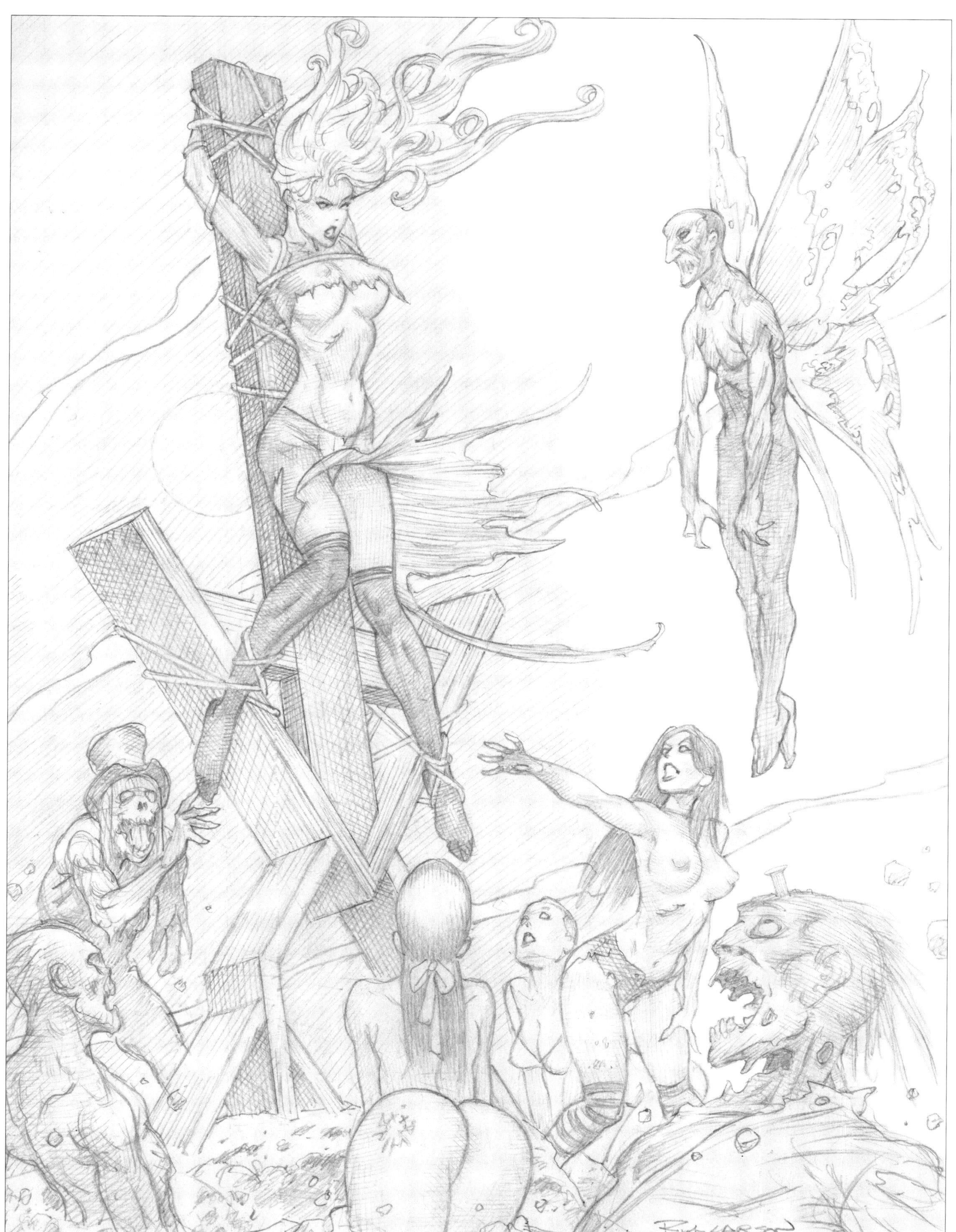

FULL MOON FEVER

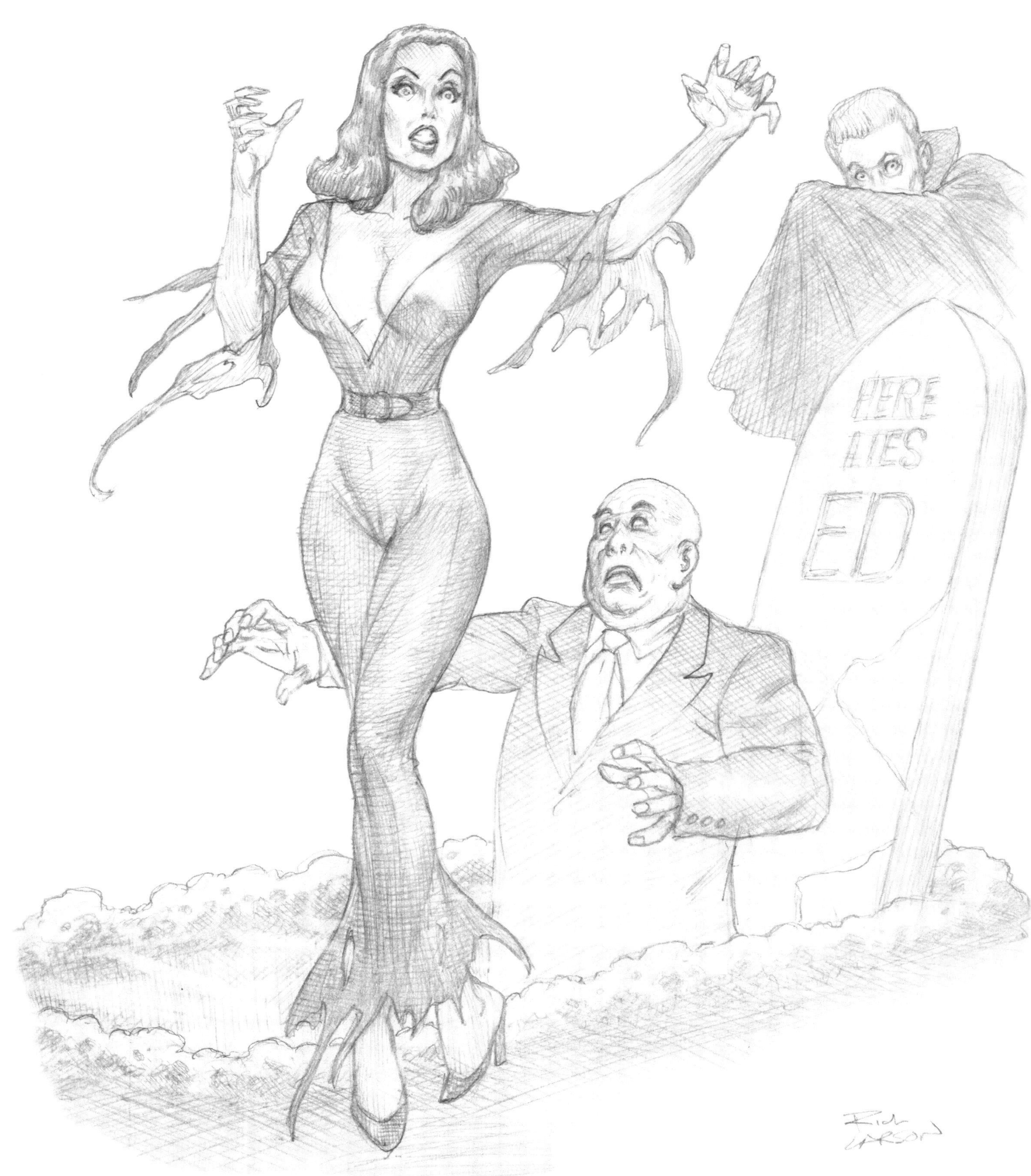

HERE LIES ED

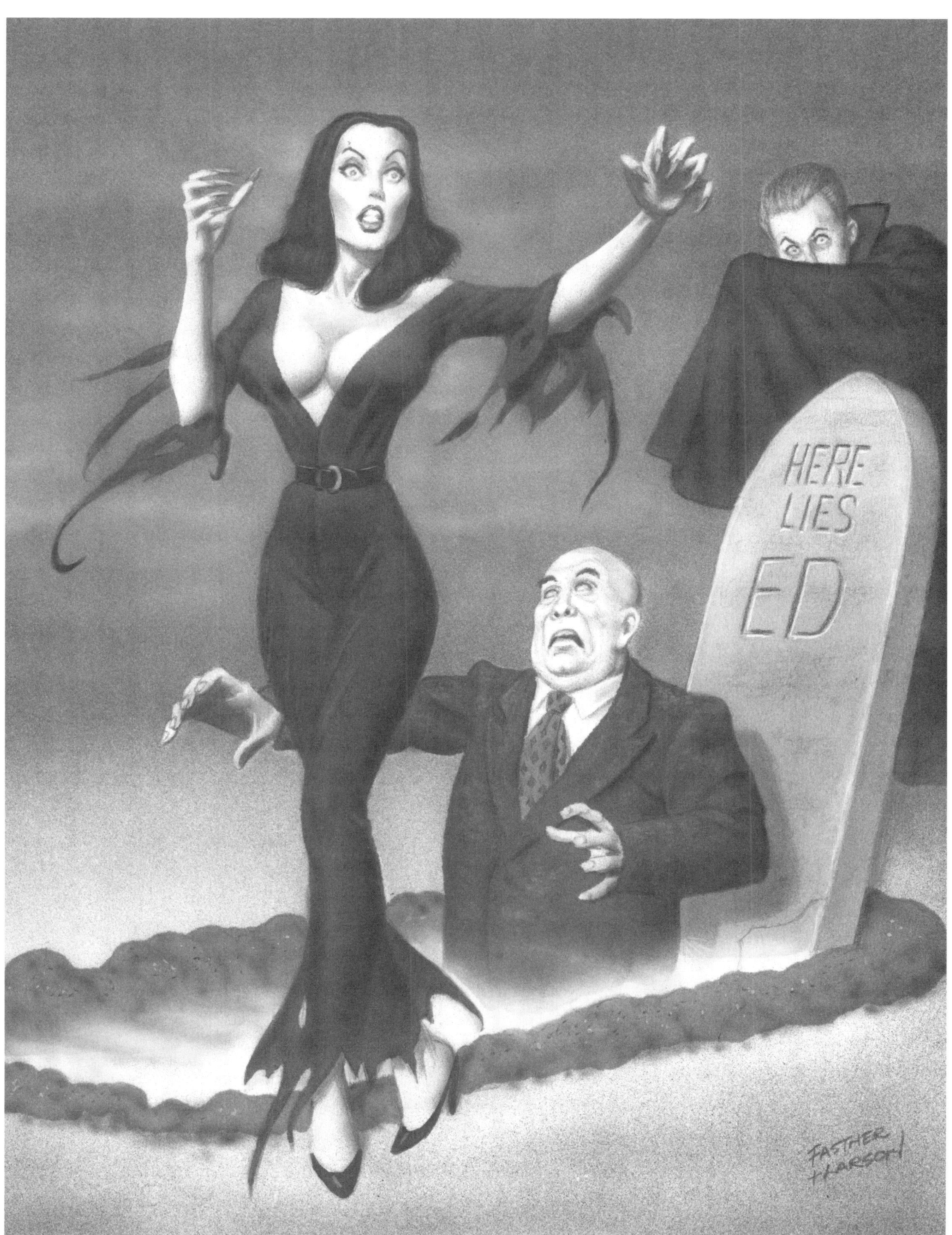

HERE LIES ED PAINTING

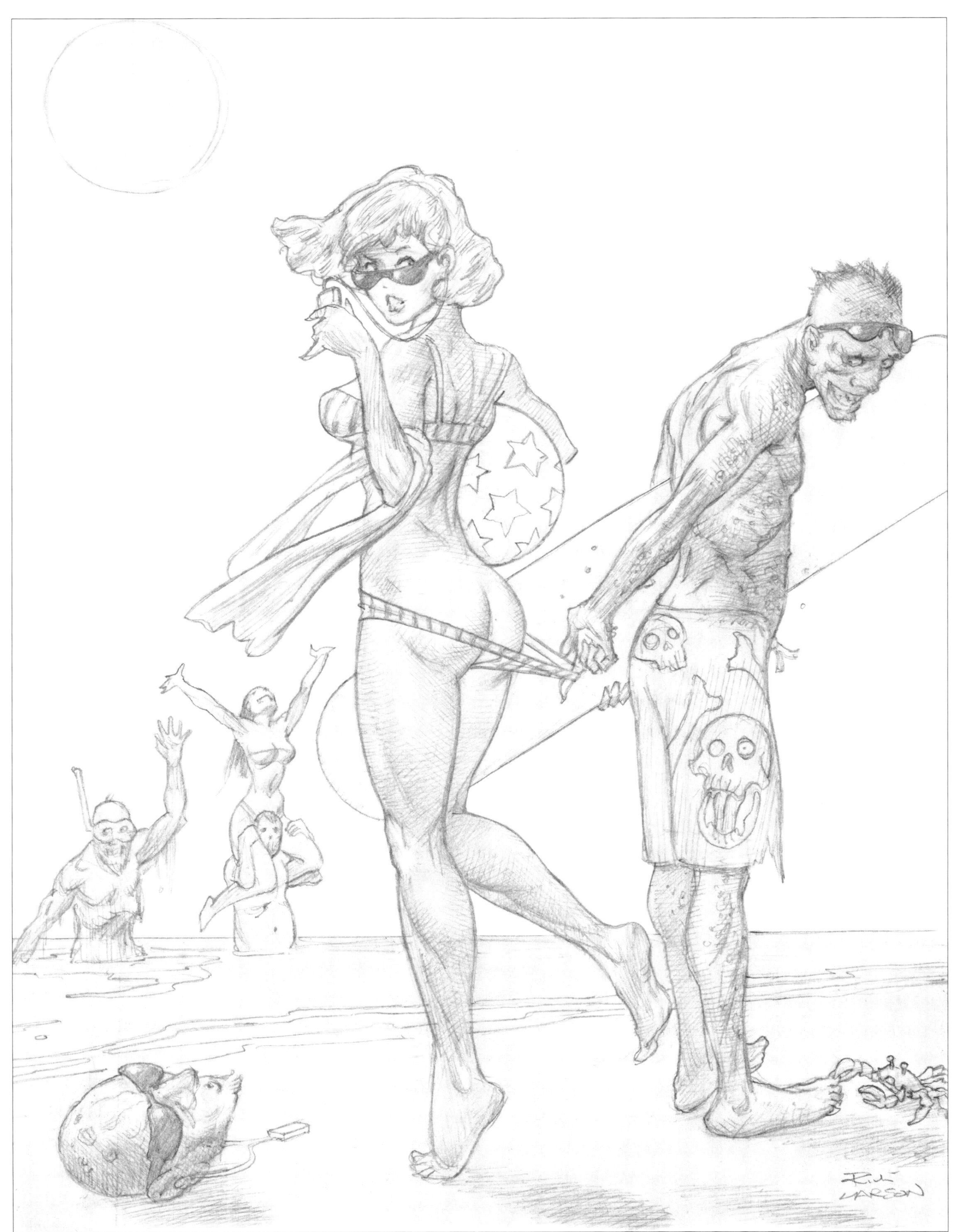

BEACH BUNNIES

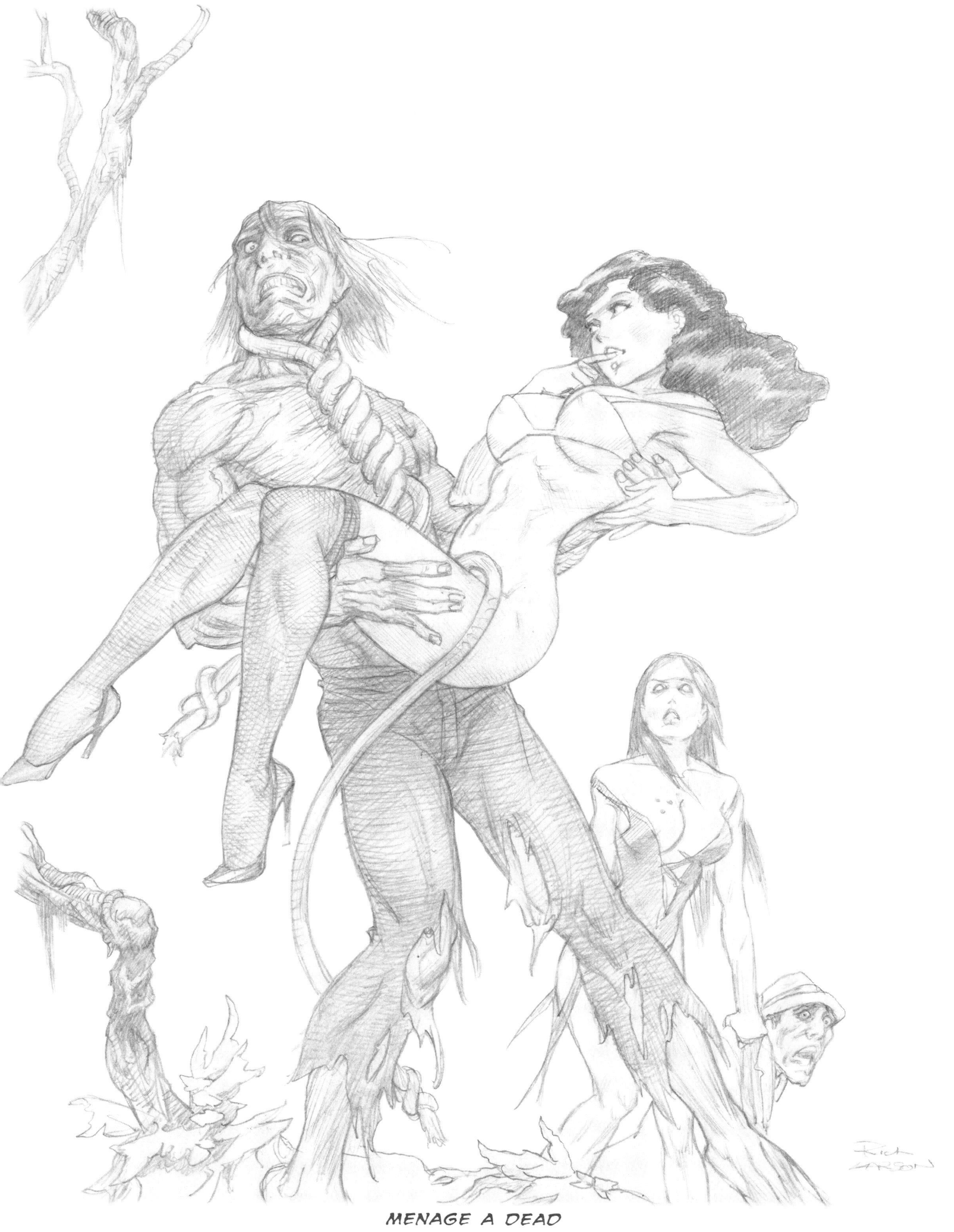

MENAGE A DEAD

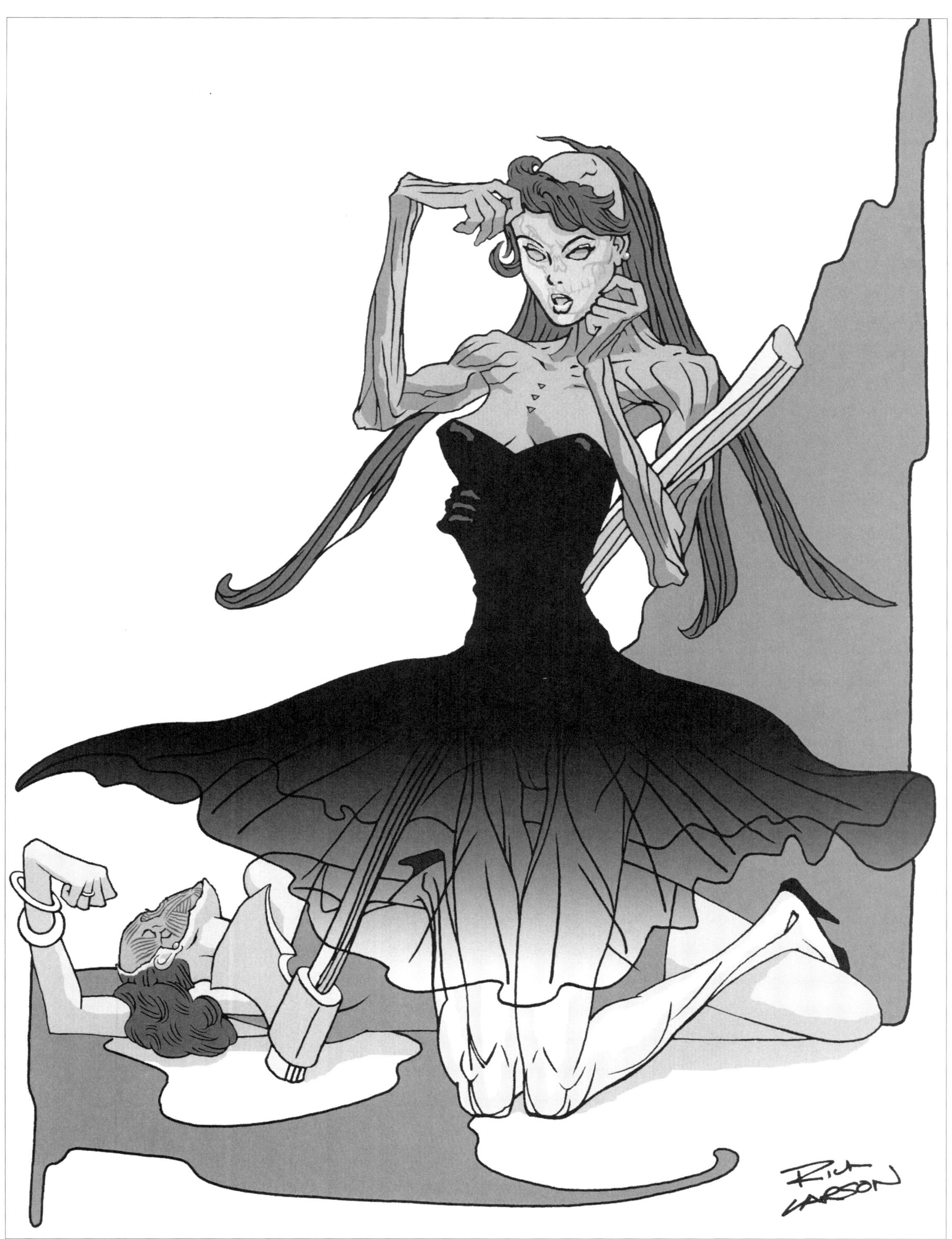

DEFACED

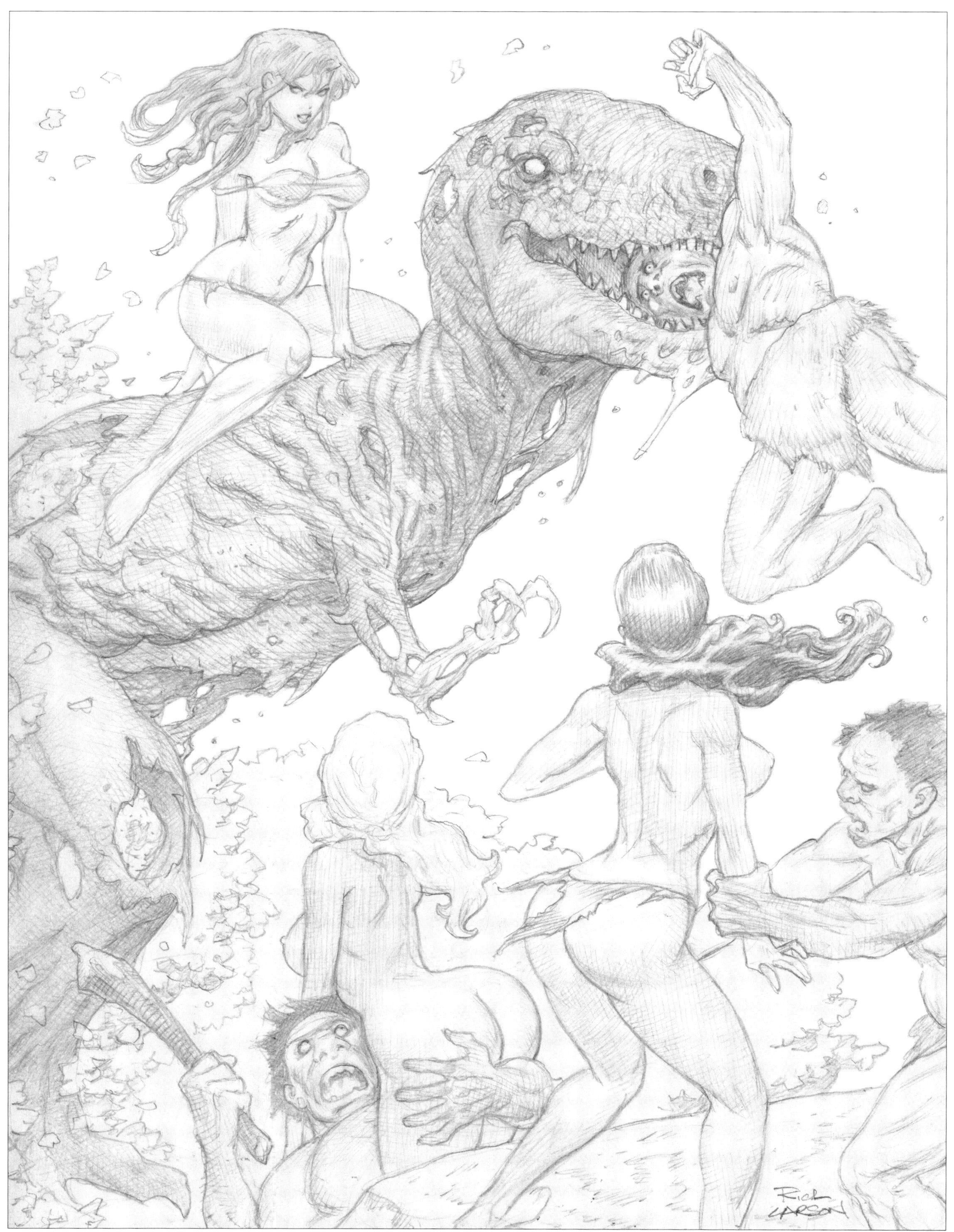

NOT QUITE EXTINCT

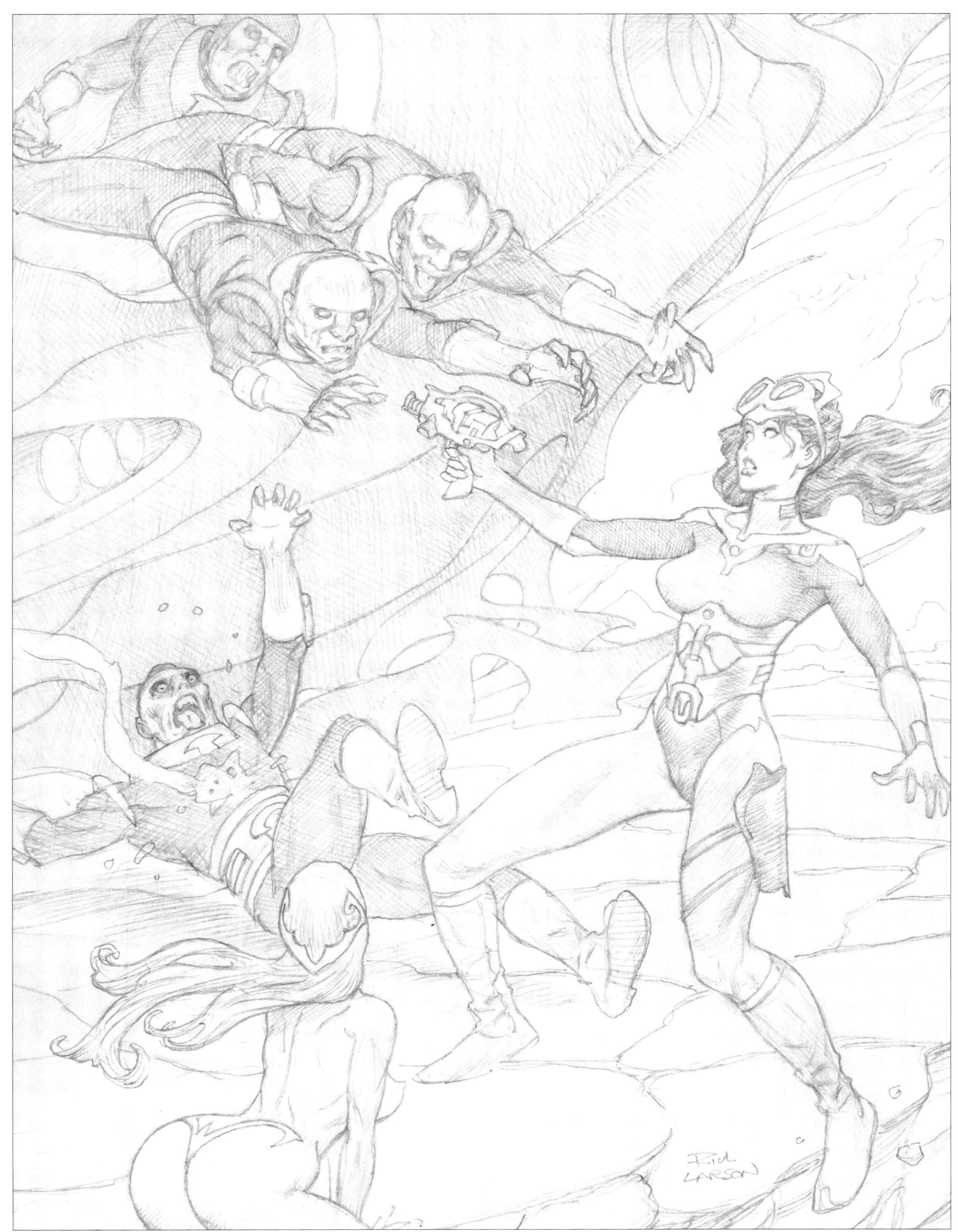

SPACE CORPSE

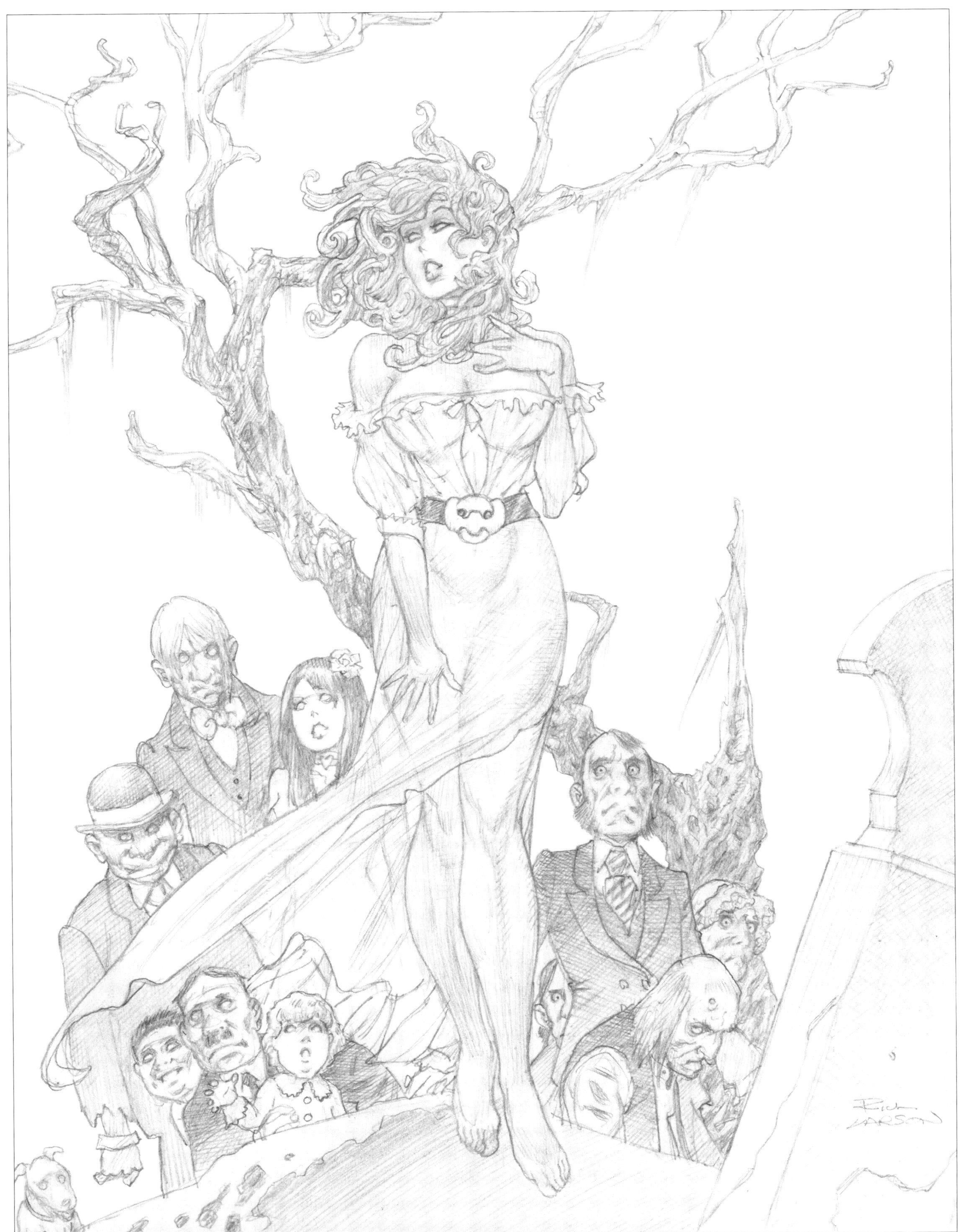

MOURNERS

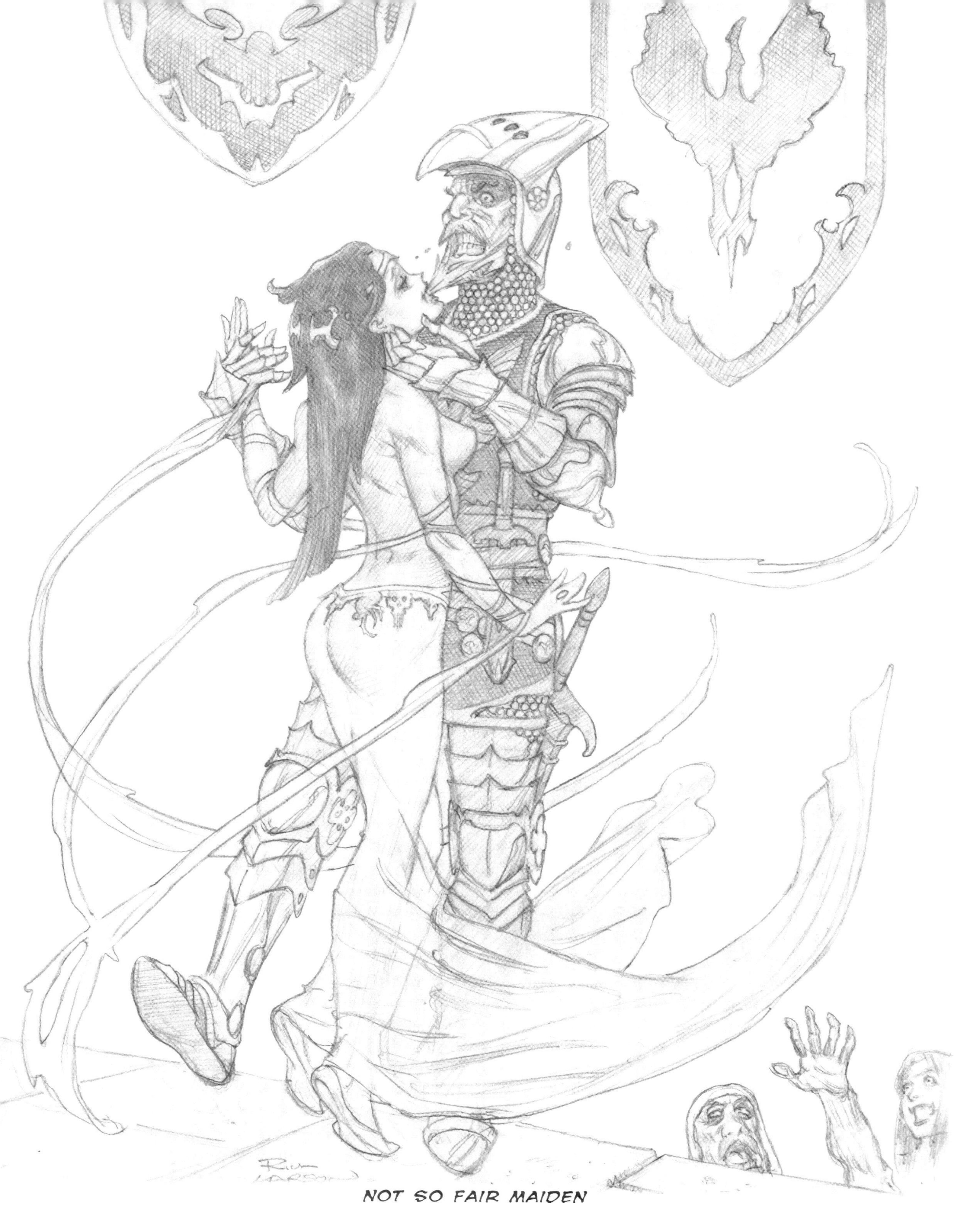

NOT SO FAIR MAIDEN

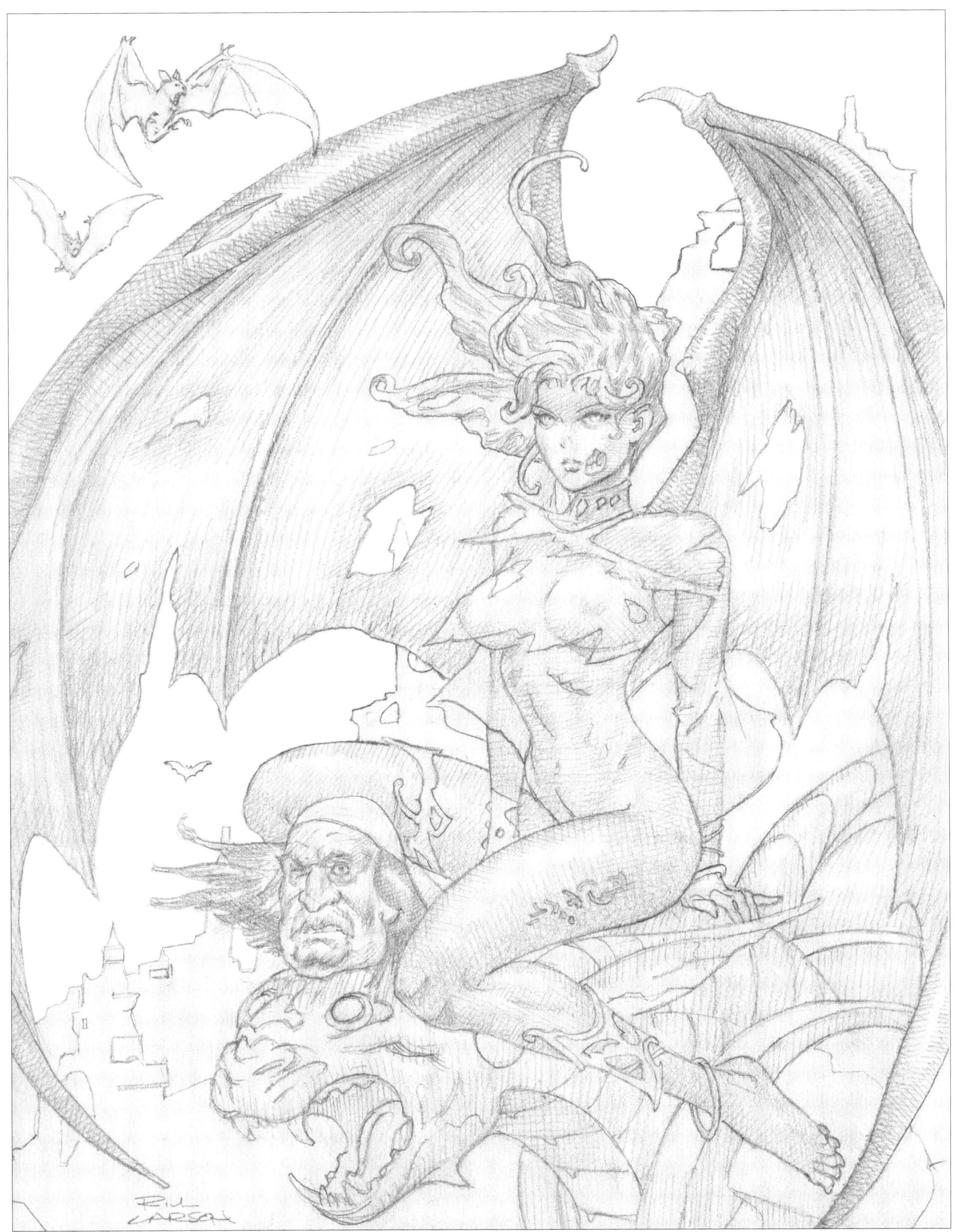

CARDINAL'S HEAD

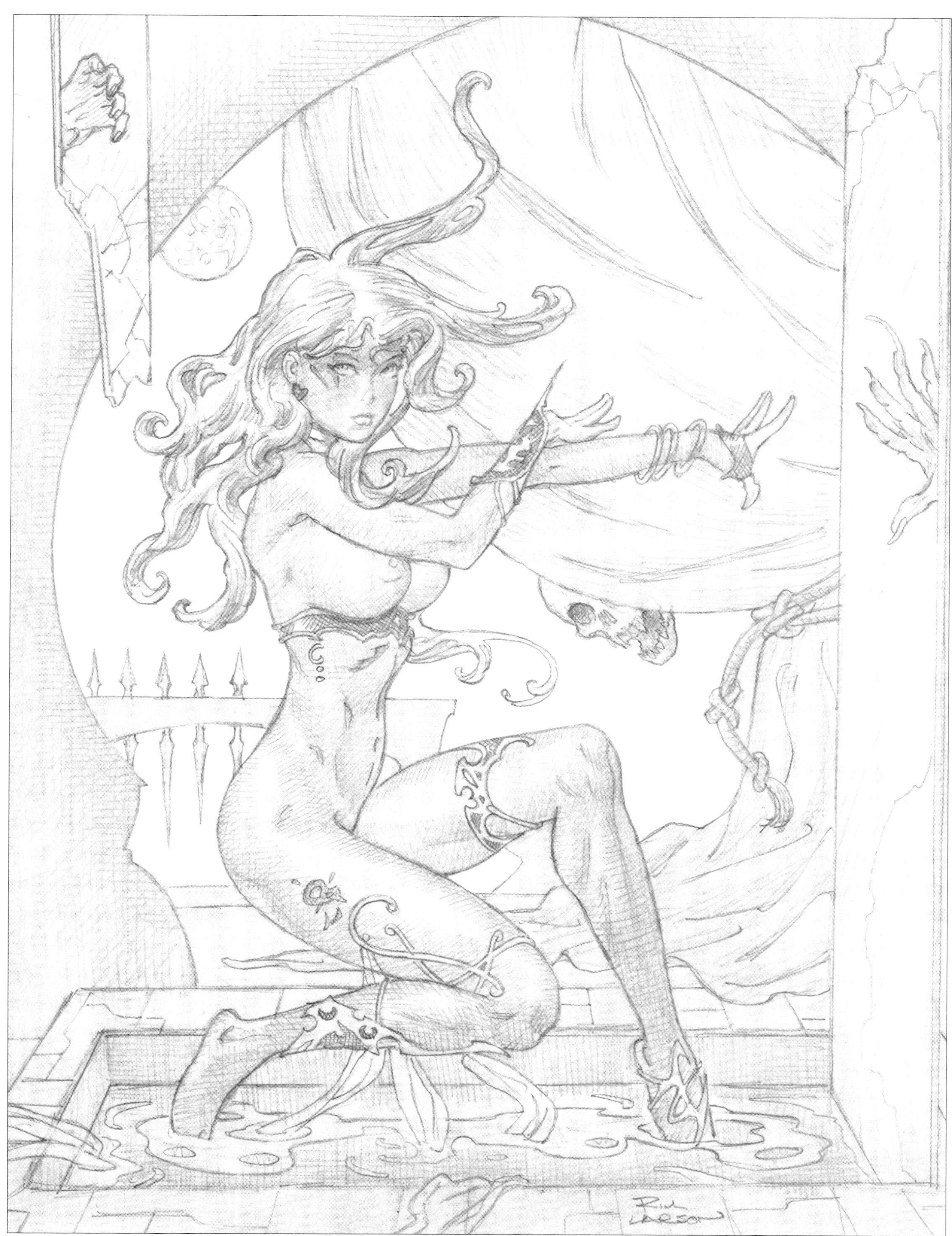

DEAD POOL

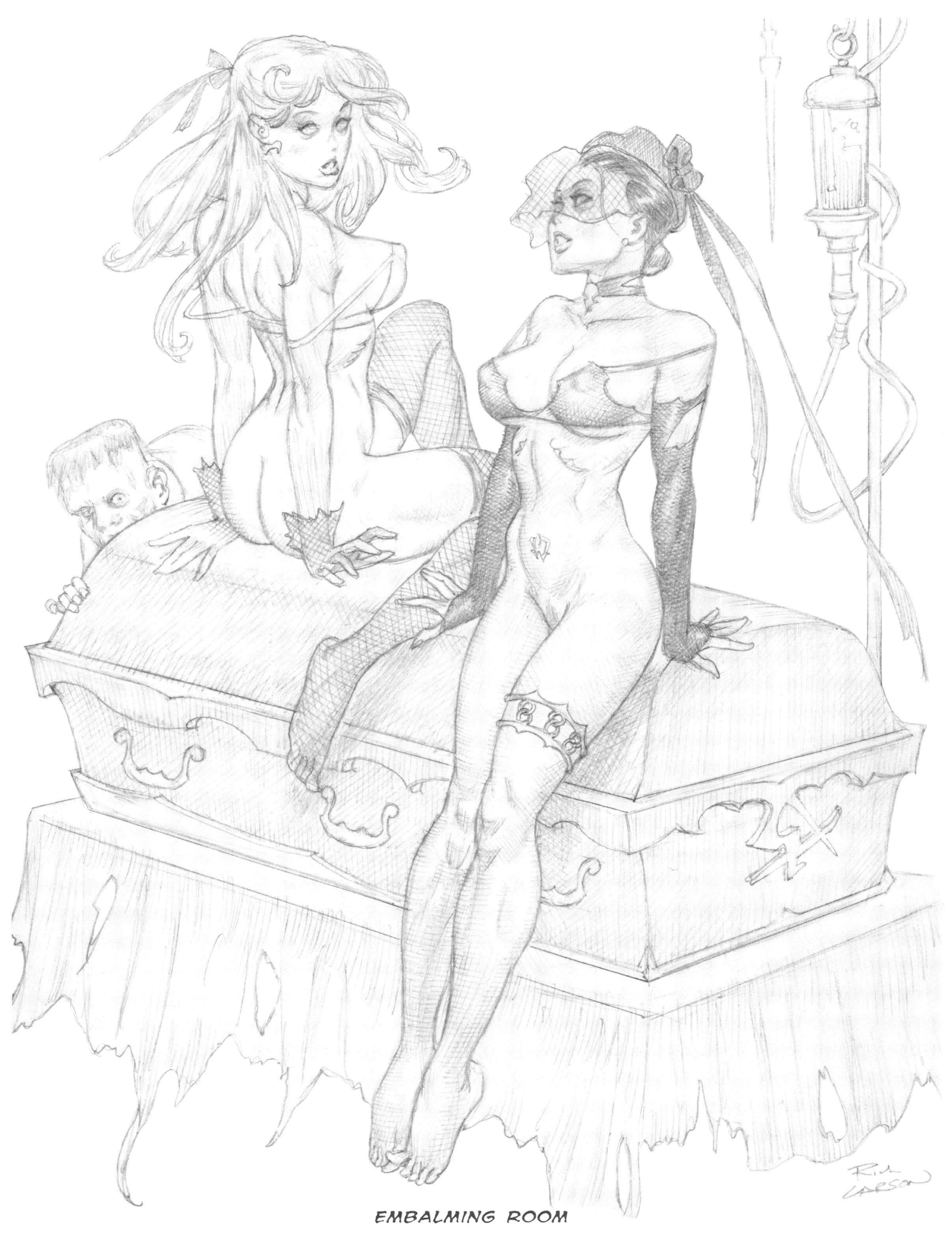

EMBALMING ROOM

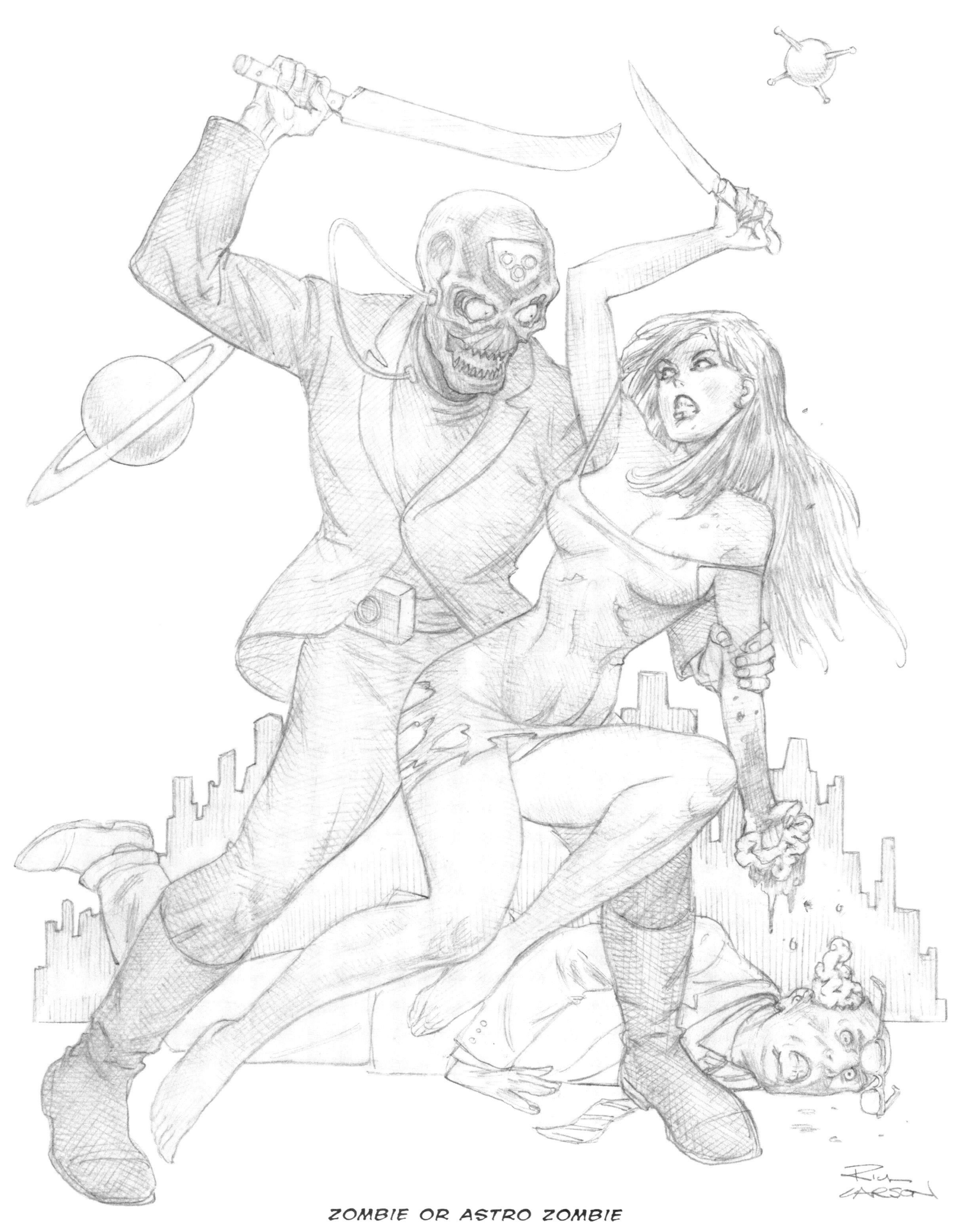

ZOMBIE OR ASTRO ZOMBIE

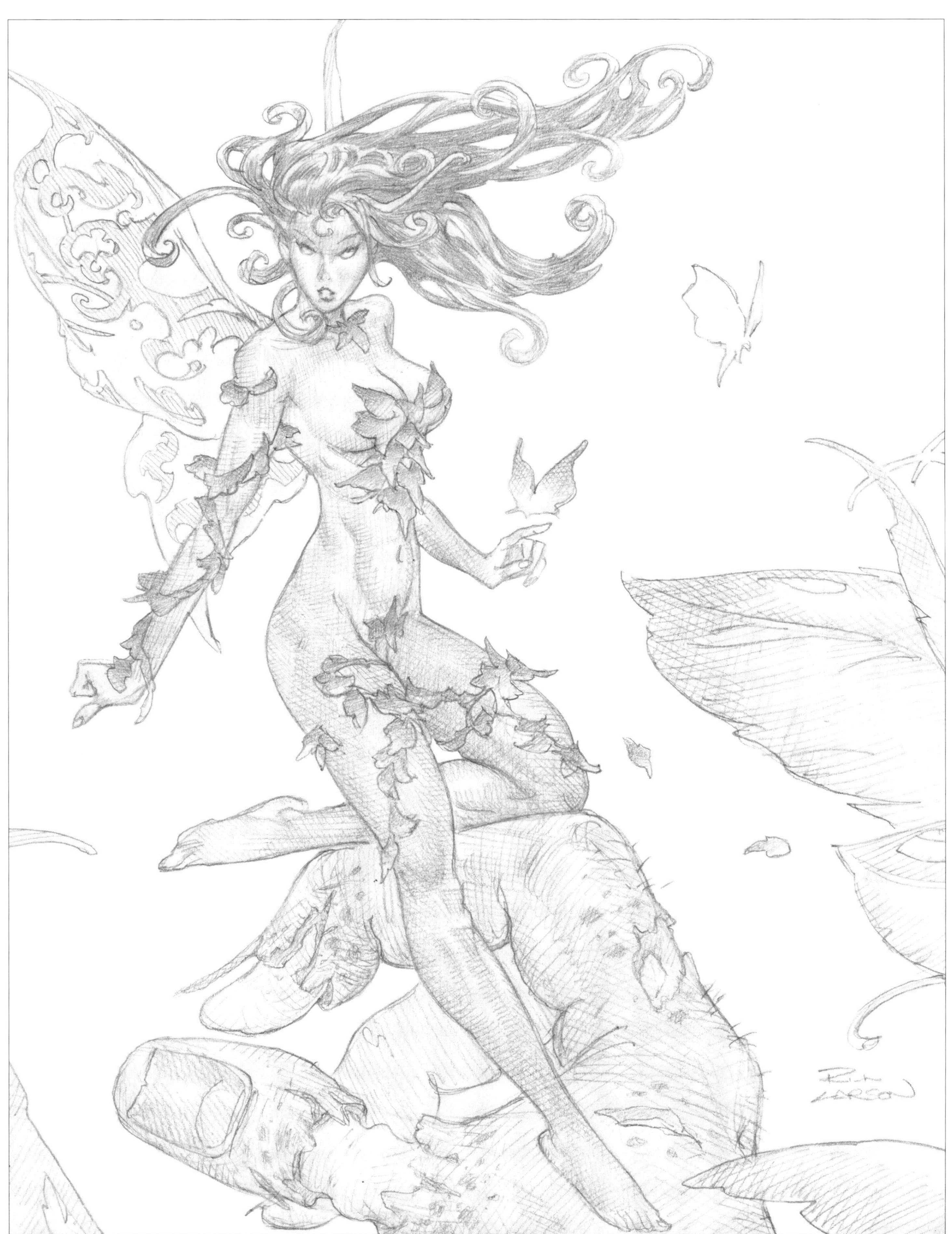

DEAD ENTOMOLOGIST

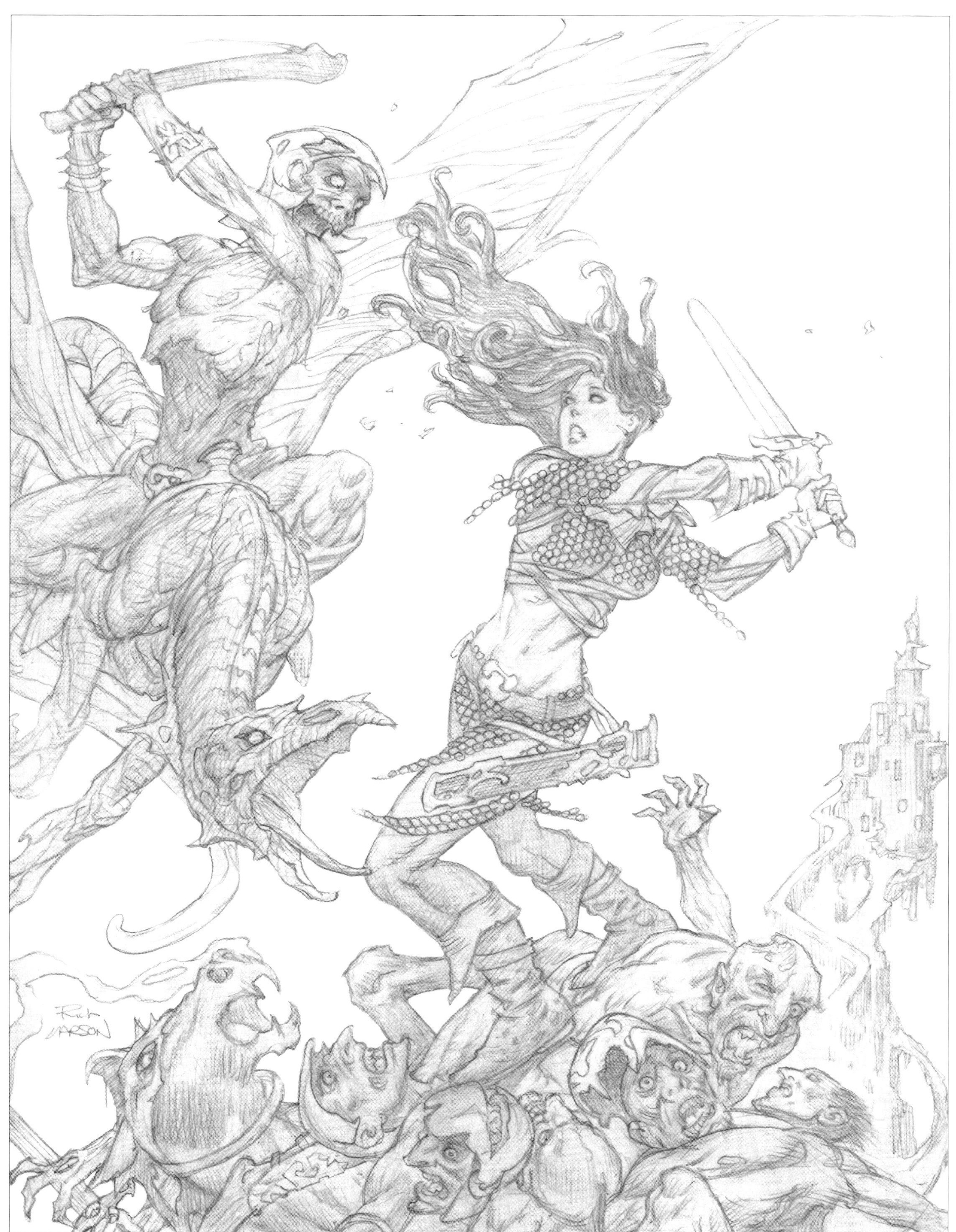

ARMIES OF THE NIGHT

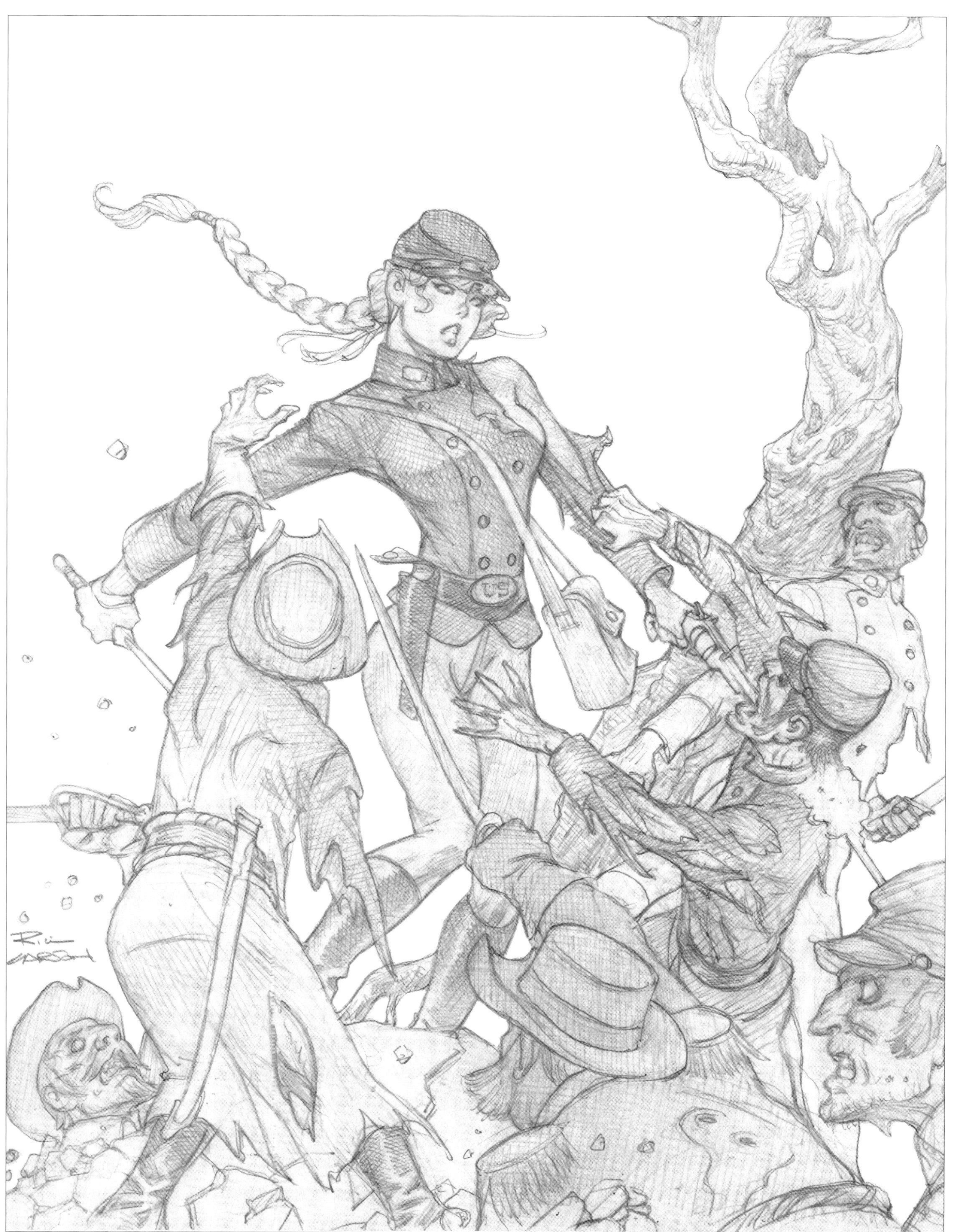

THE SOUTH SHALL RISE AGAIN

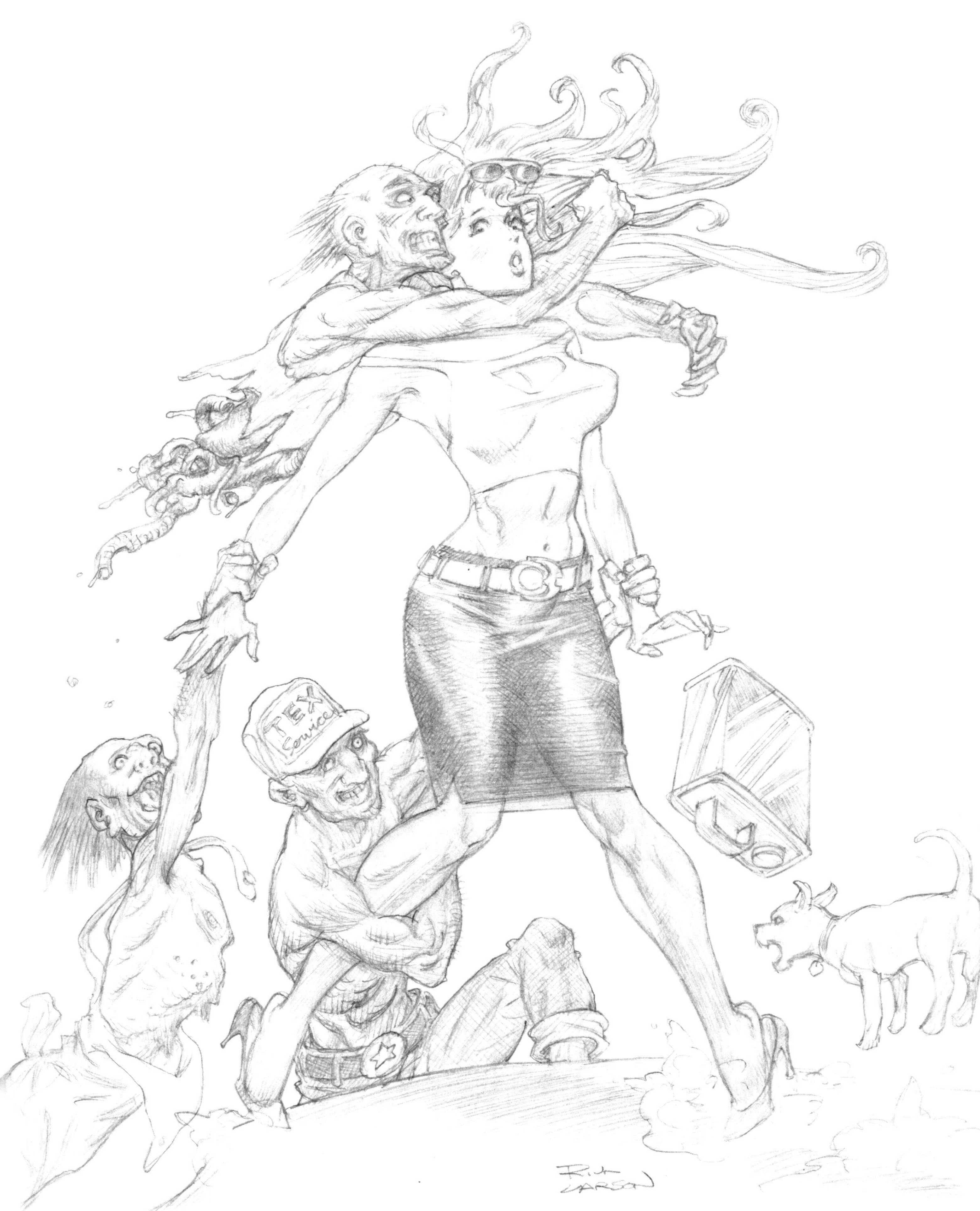

OUT OF GAS

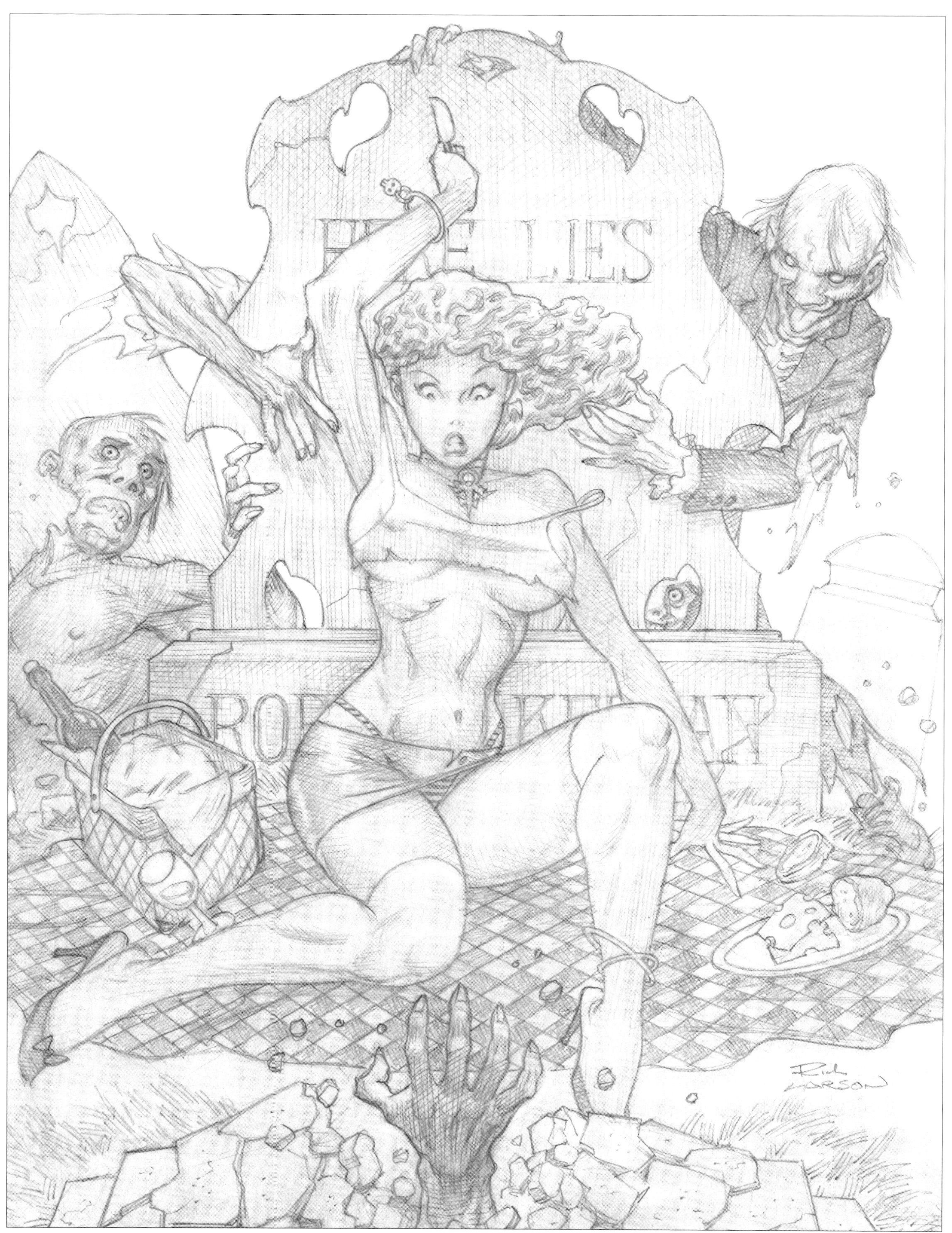

LIKE ANTS WEREN'T BAD ENOUGH

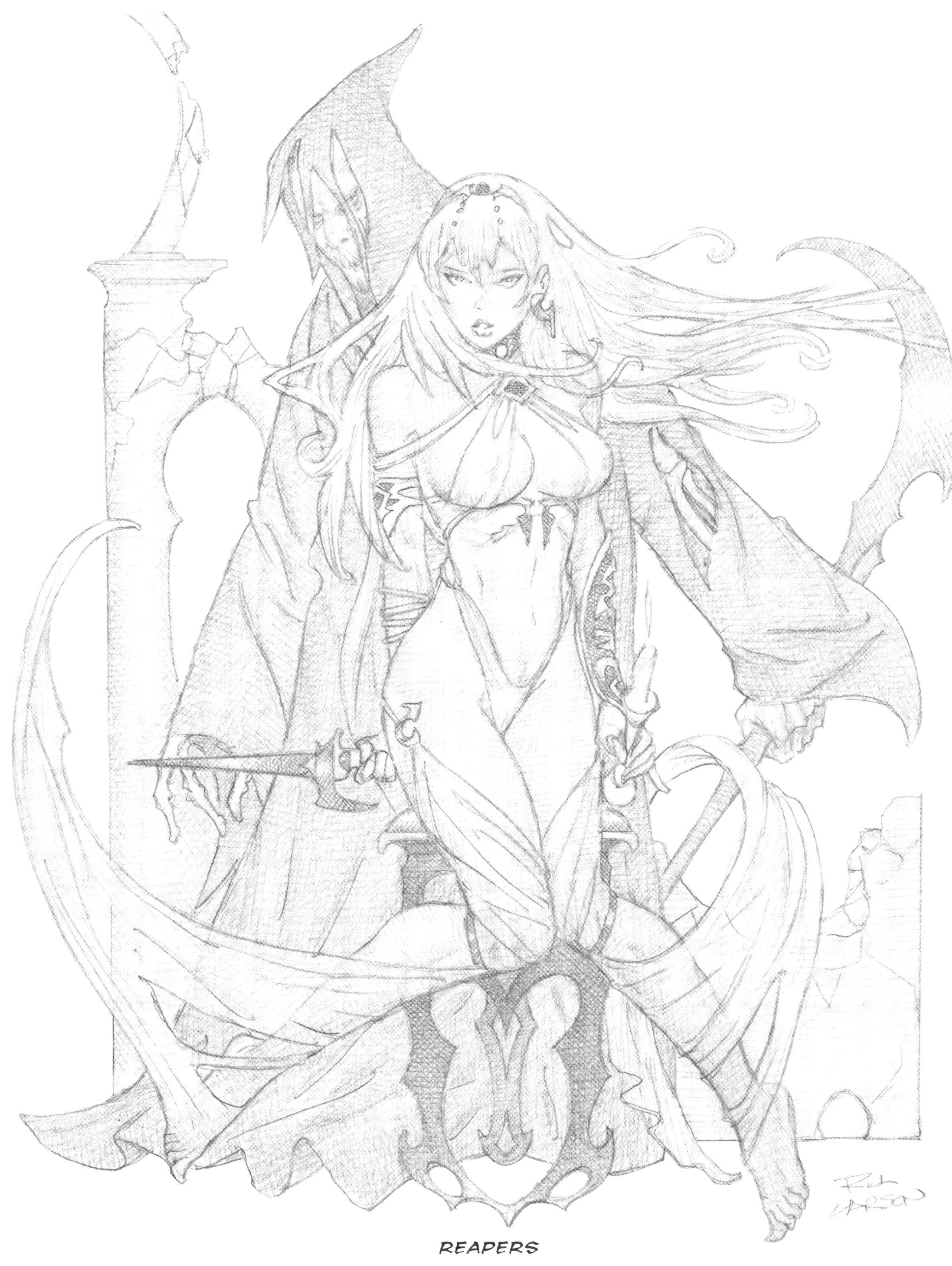

REAPERS

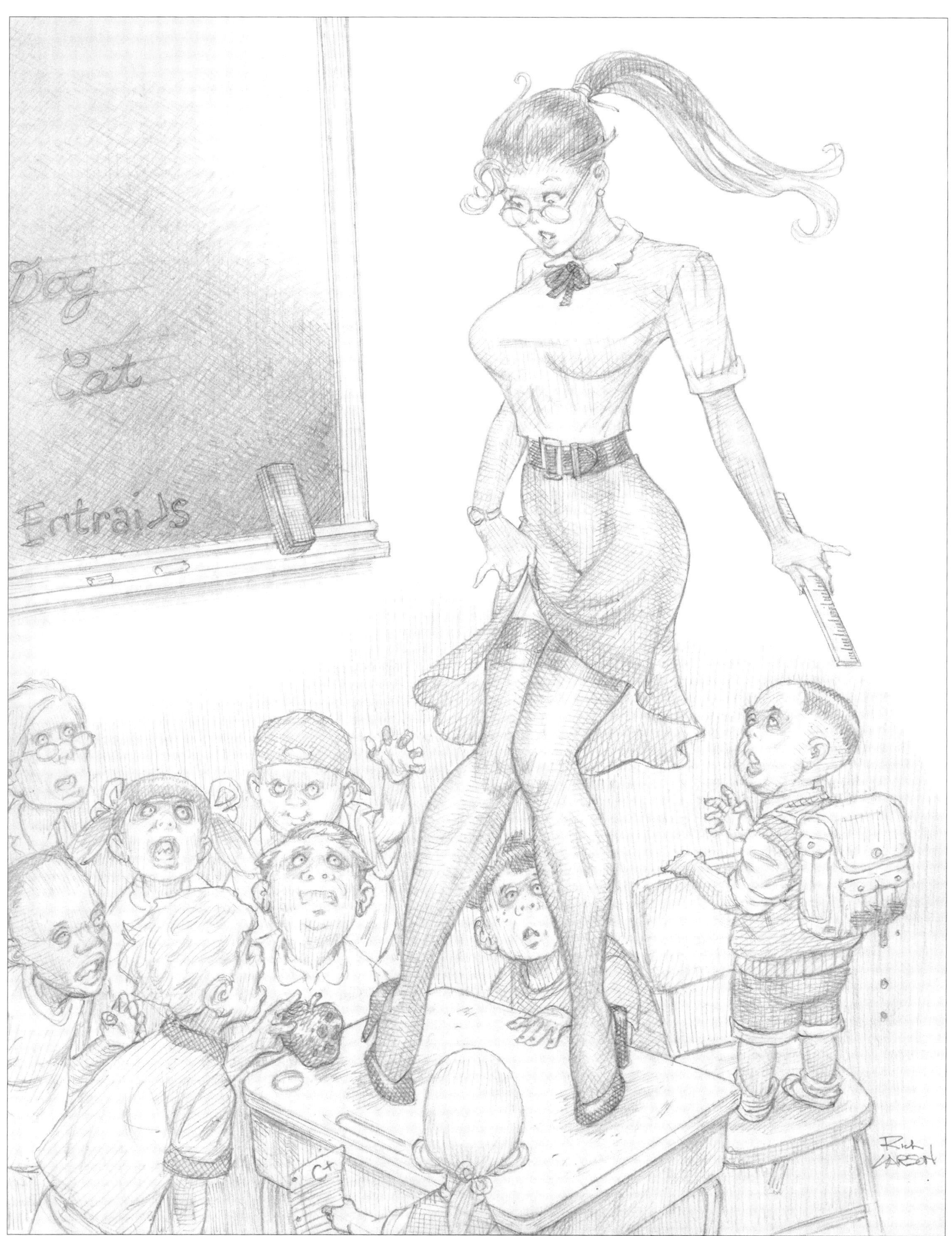

HOT FOR TEACHER

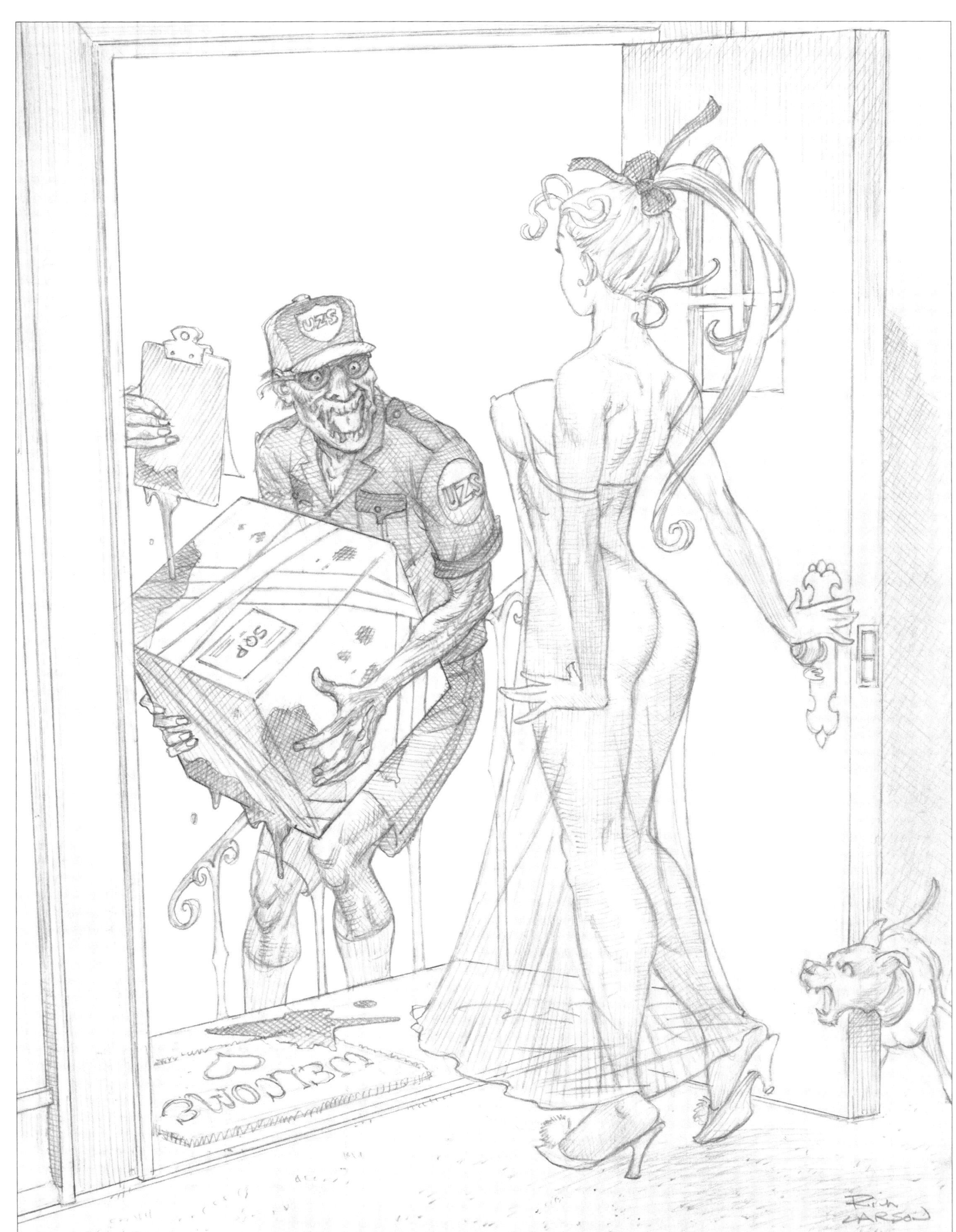

SPECIAL DELIVERY

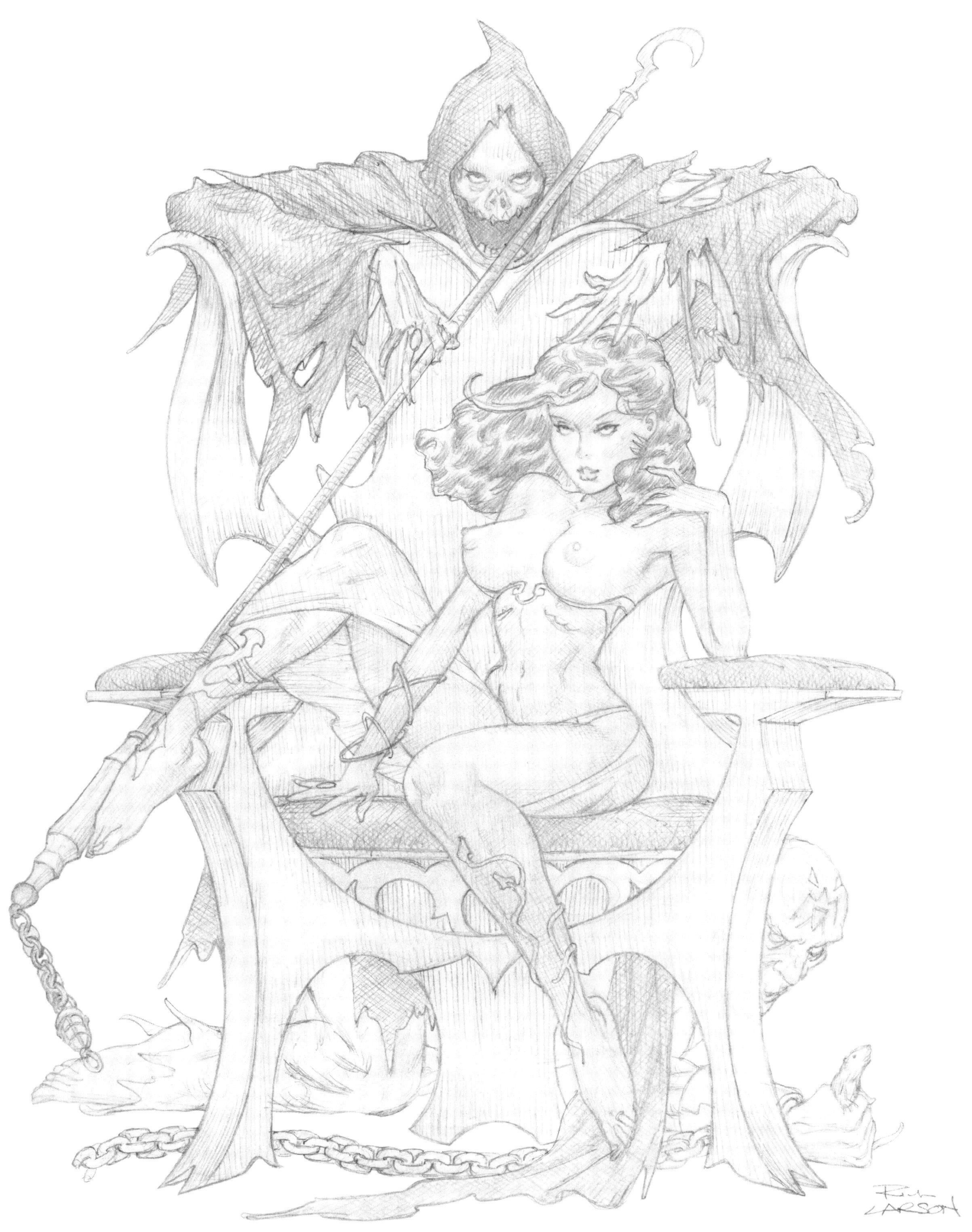

COLD SEAT

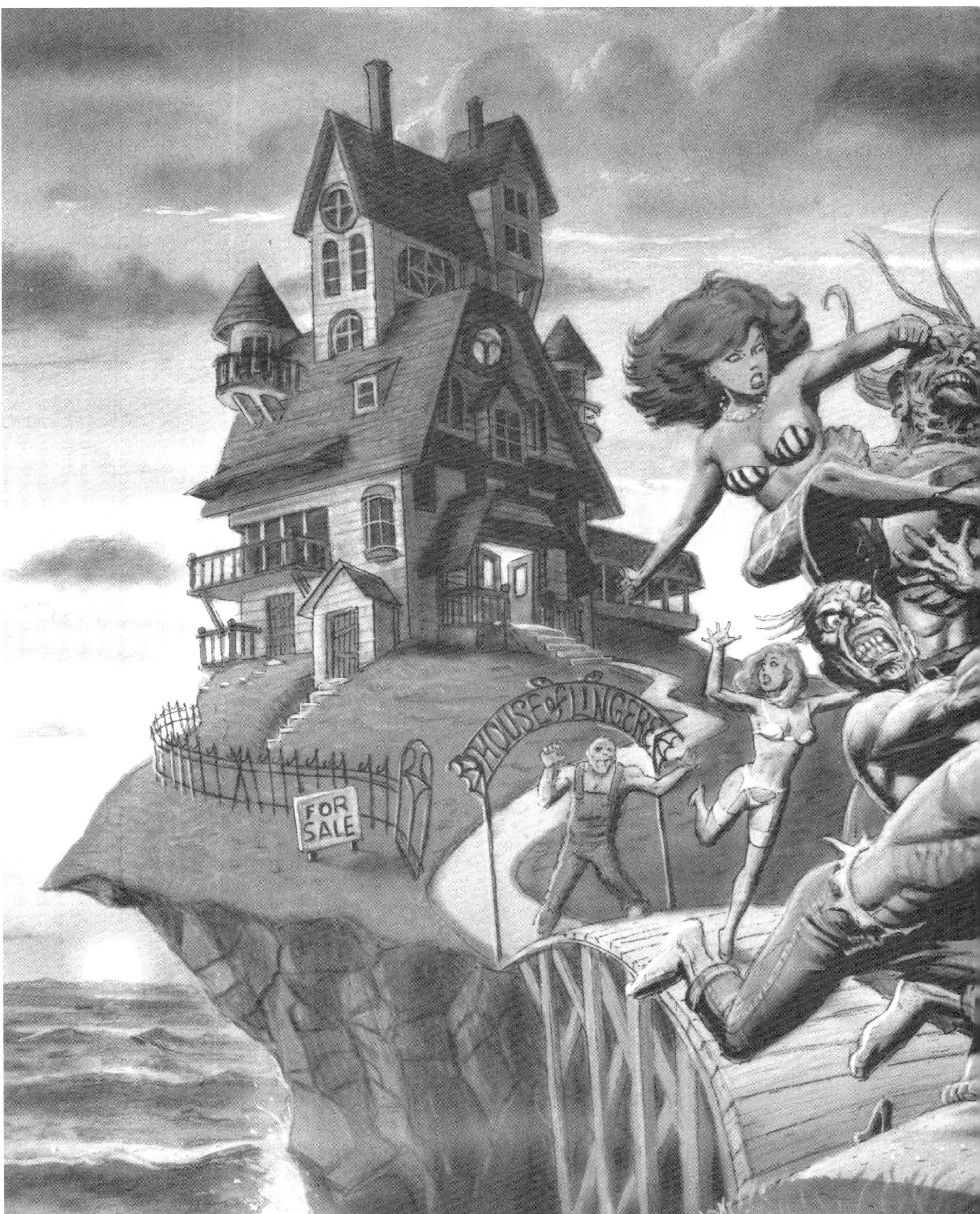
FOR
SALE

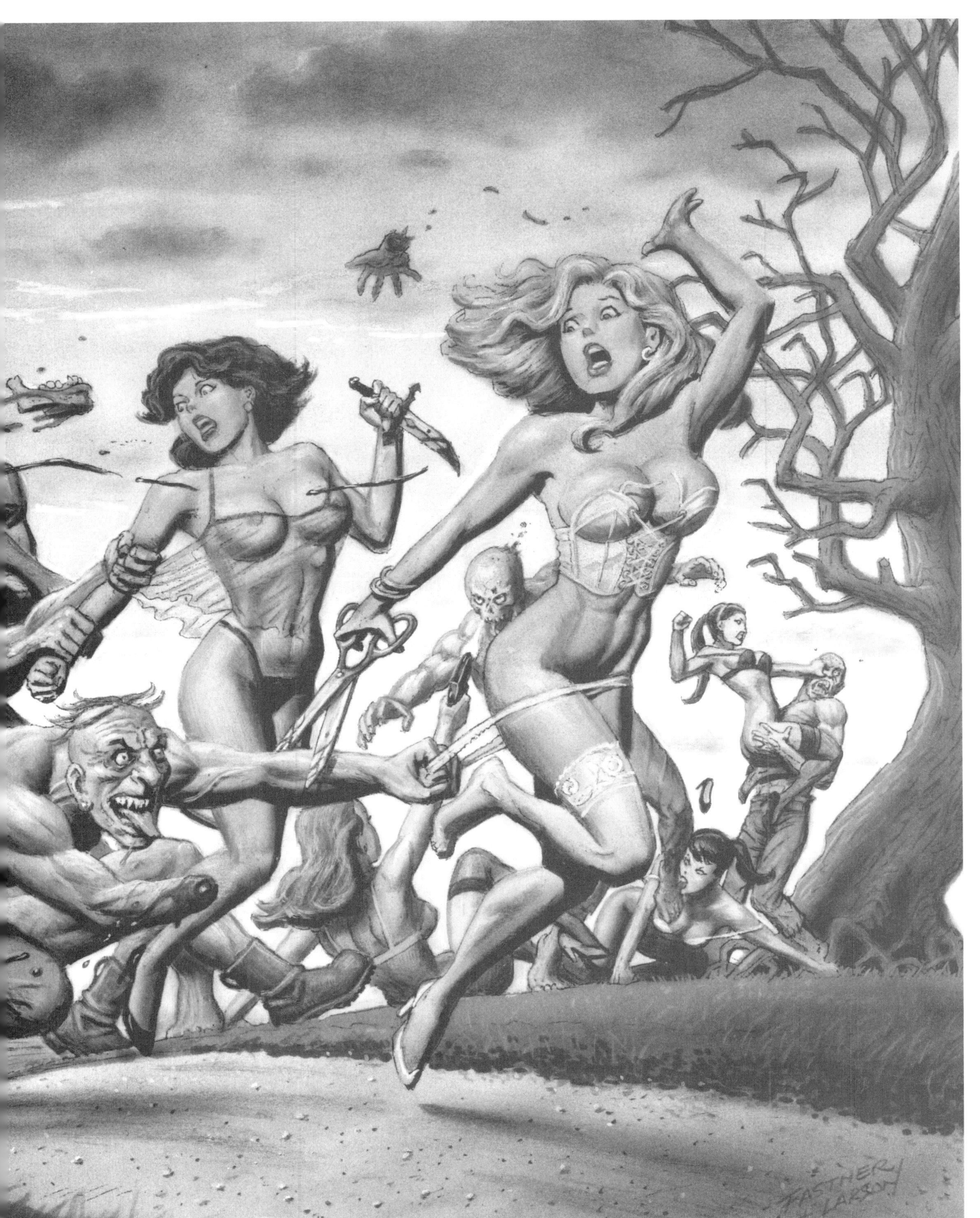

PAJAMA PARTY TONE STUDY

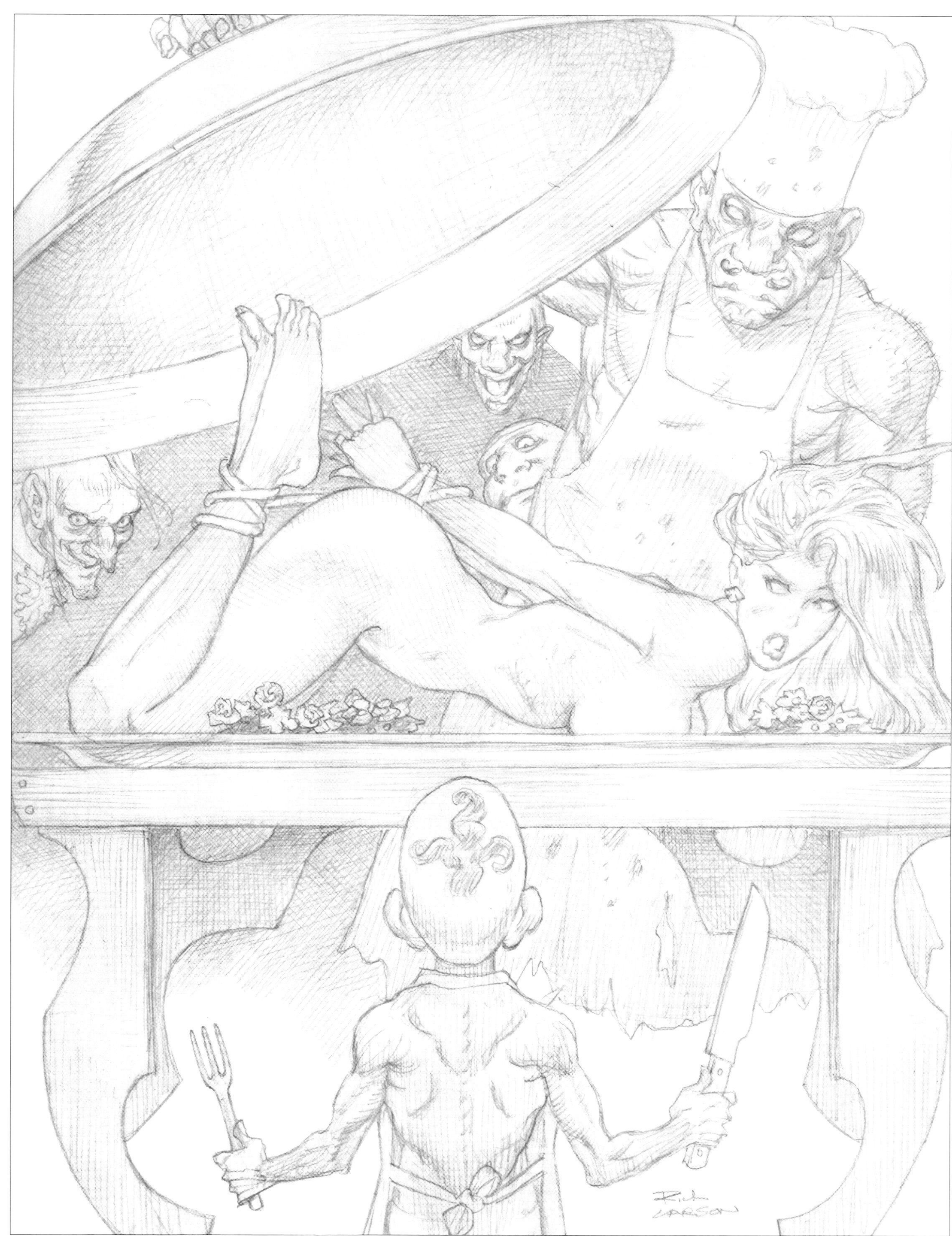

MASTER CARVER

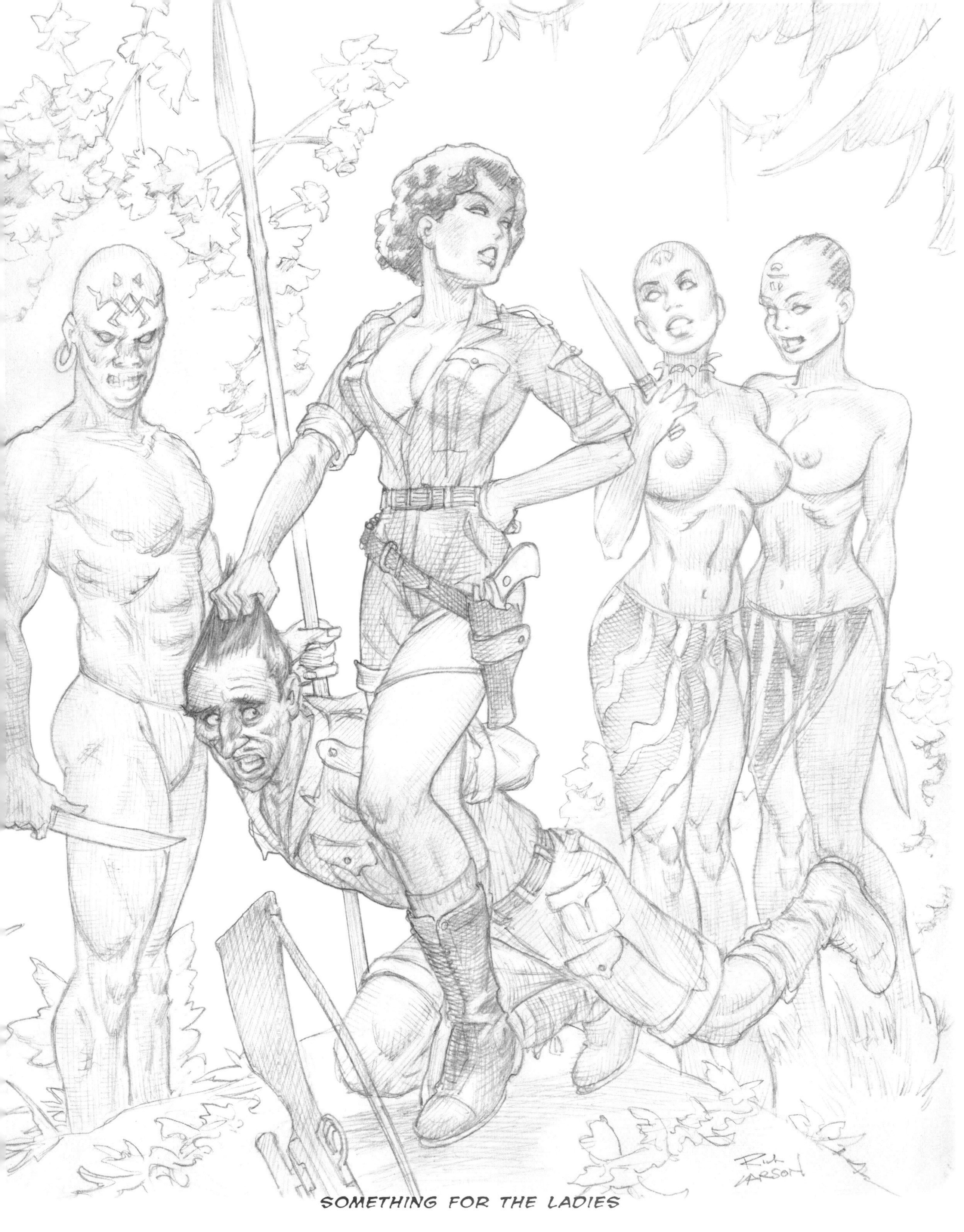

SOMETHING FOR THE LADIES

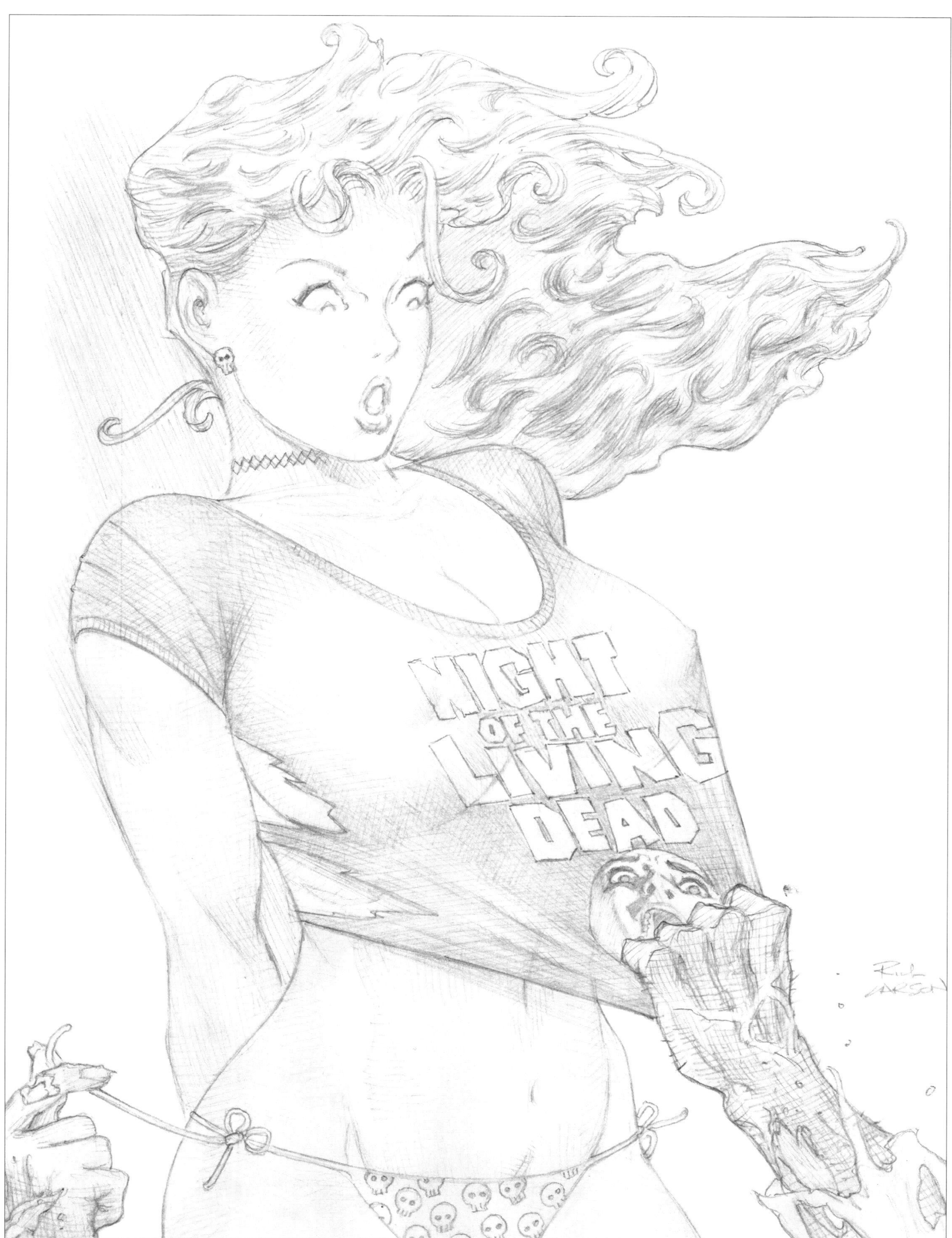

NIGHT T

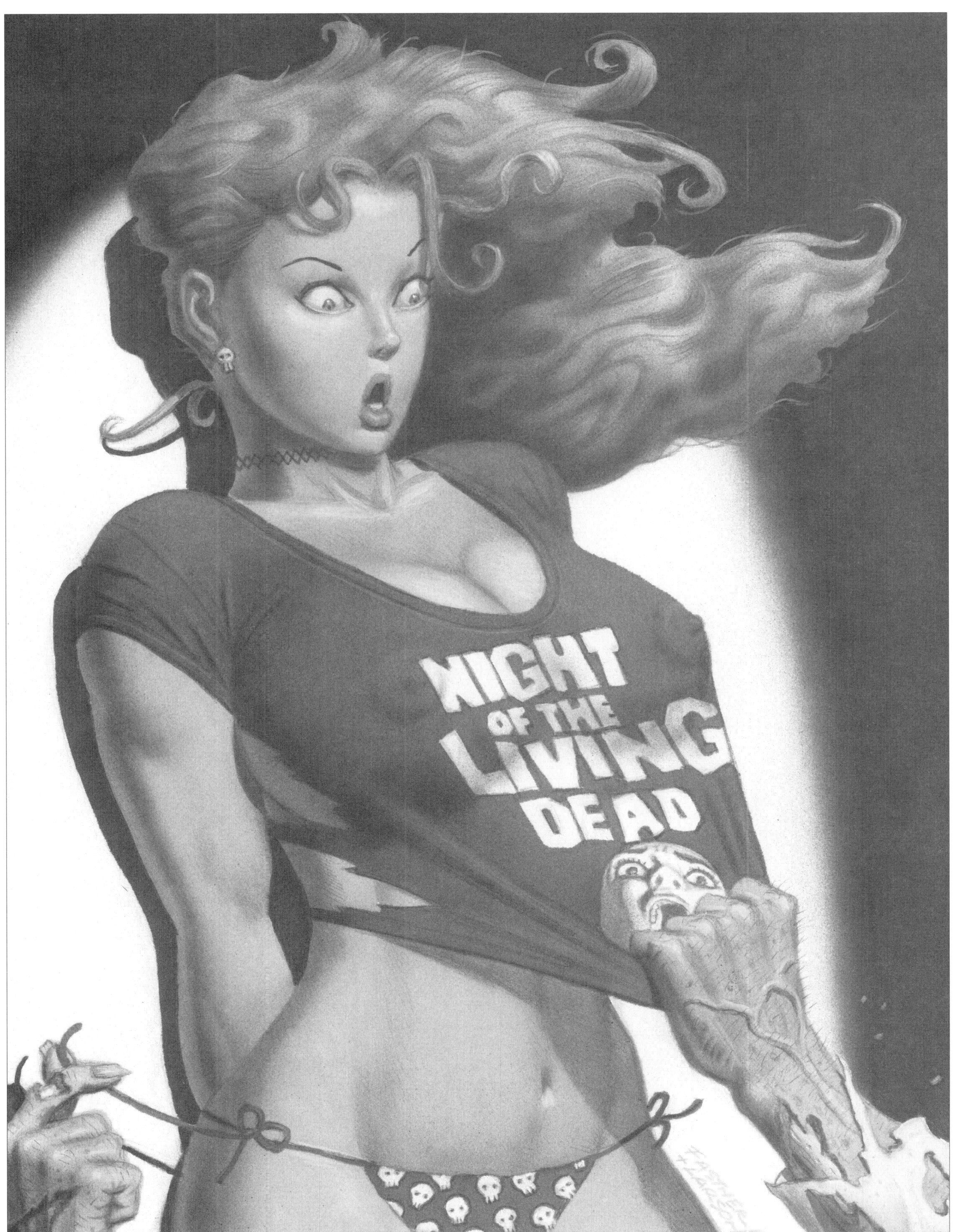

NIGHT T PAINTING

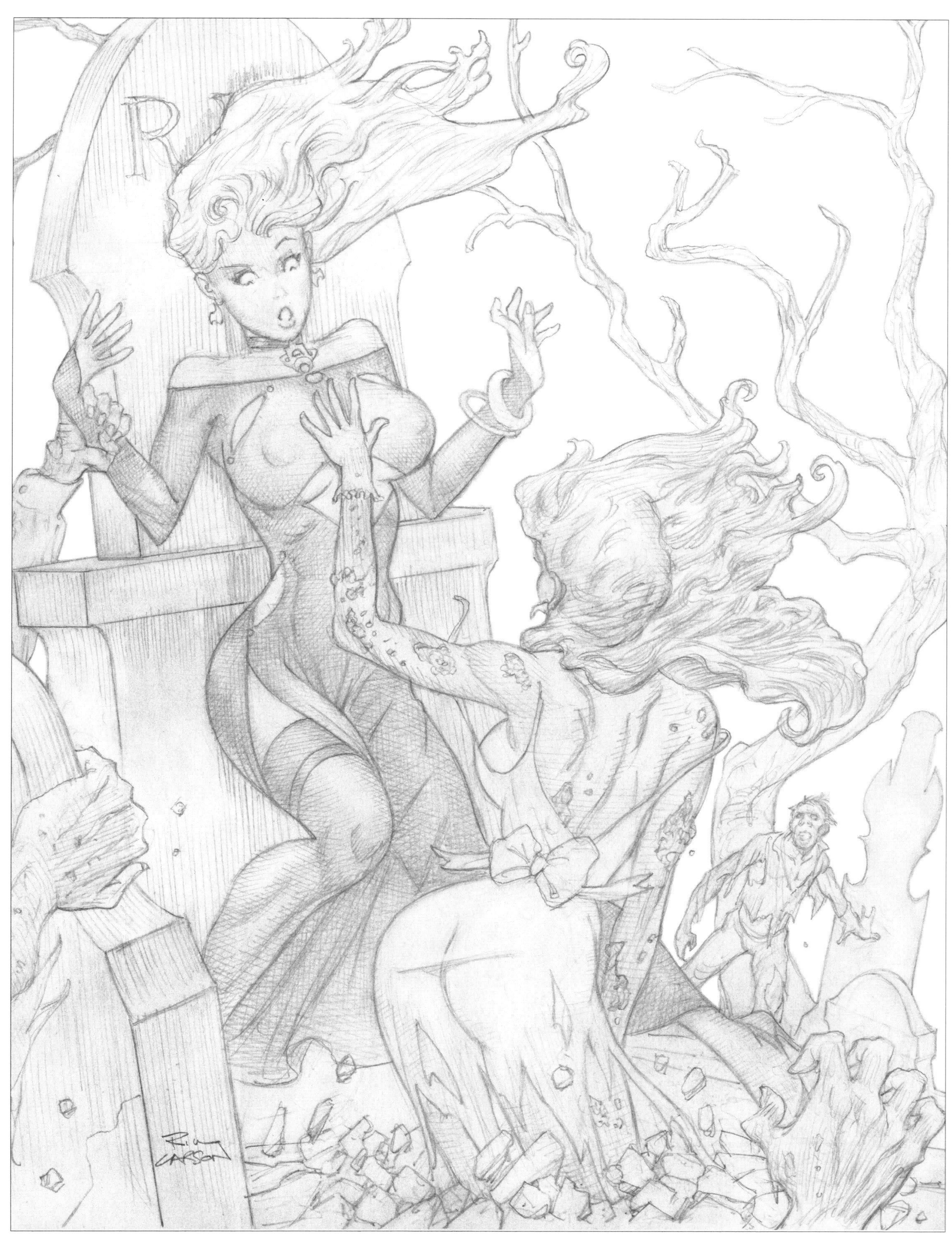

STRANGE ATTRACTION

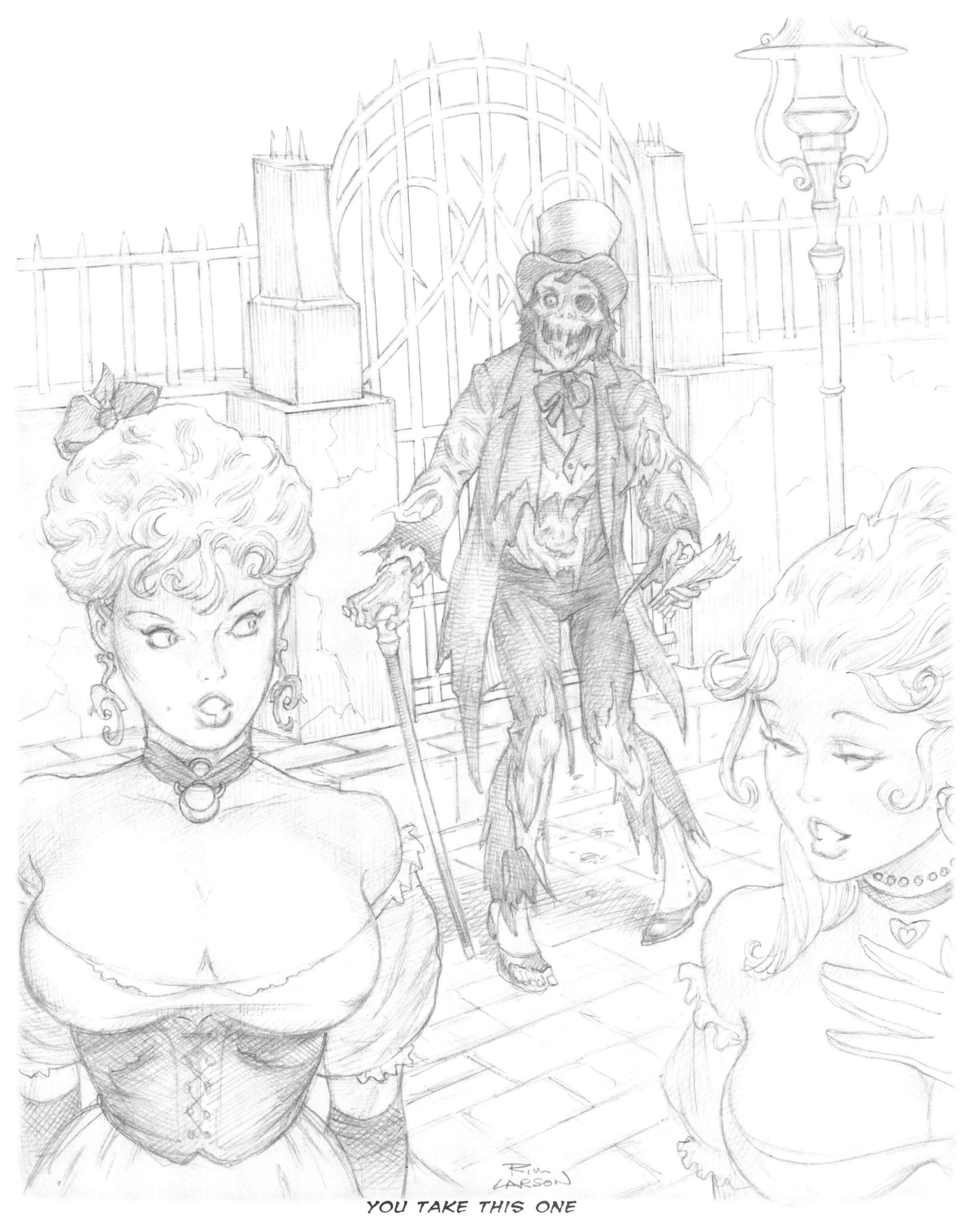

YOU TAKE THIS ONE

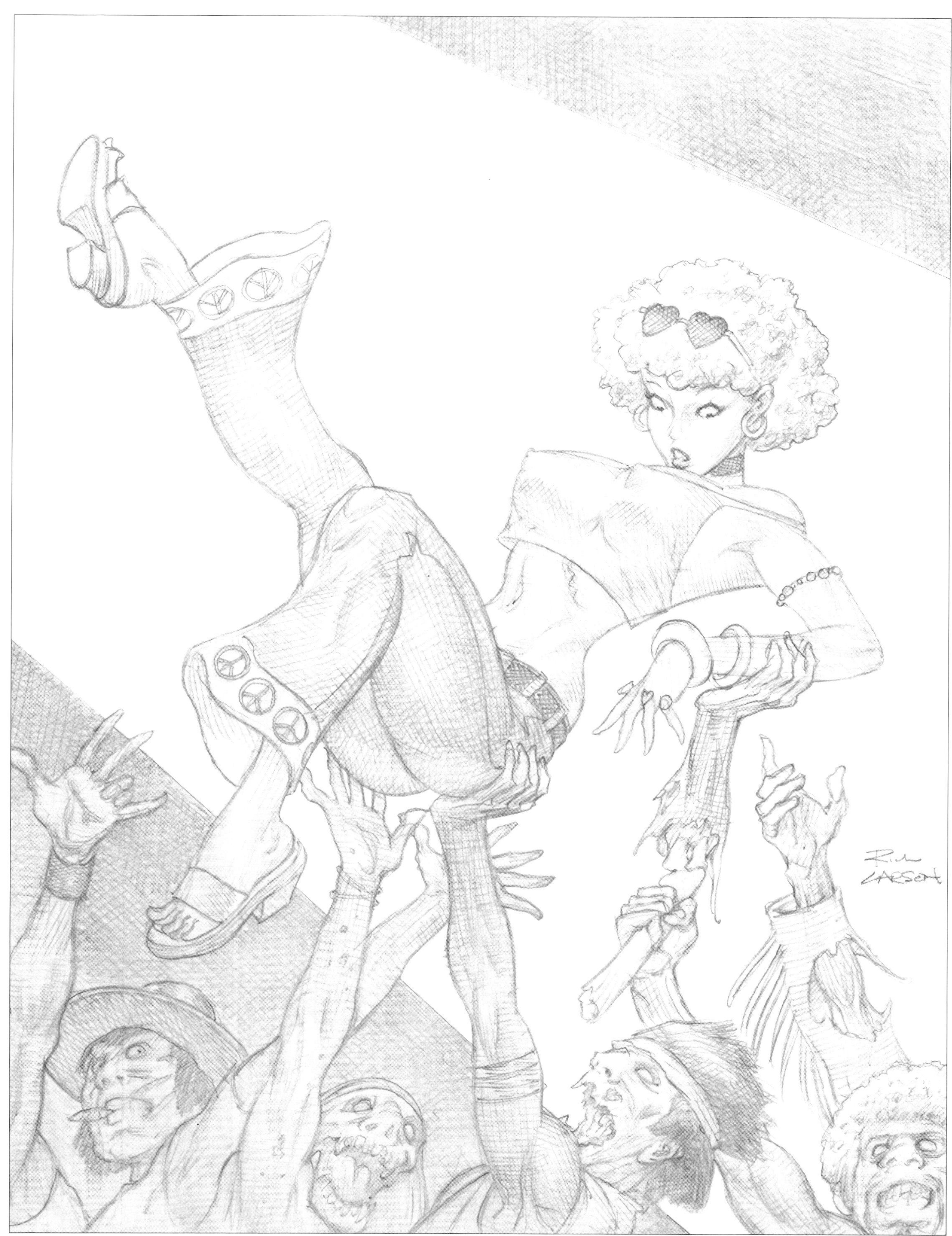

DEAD HEADS

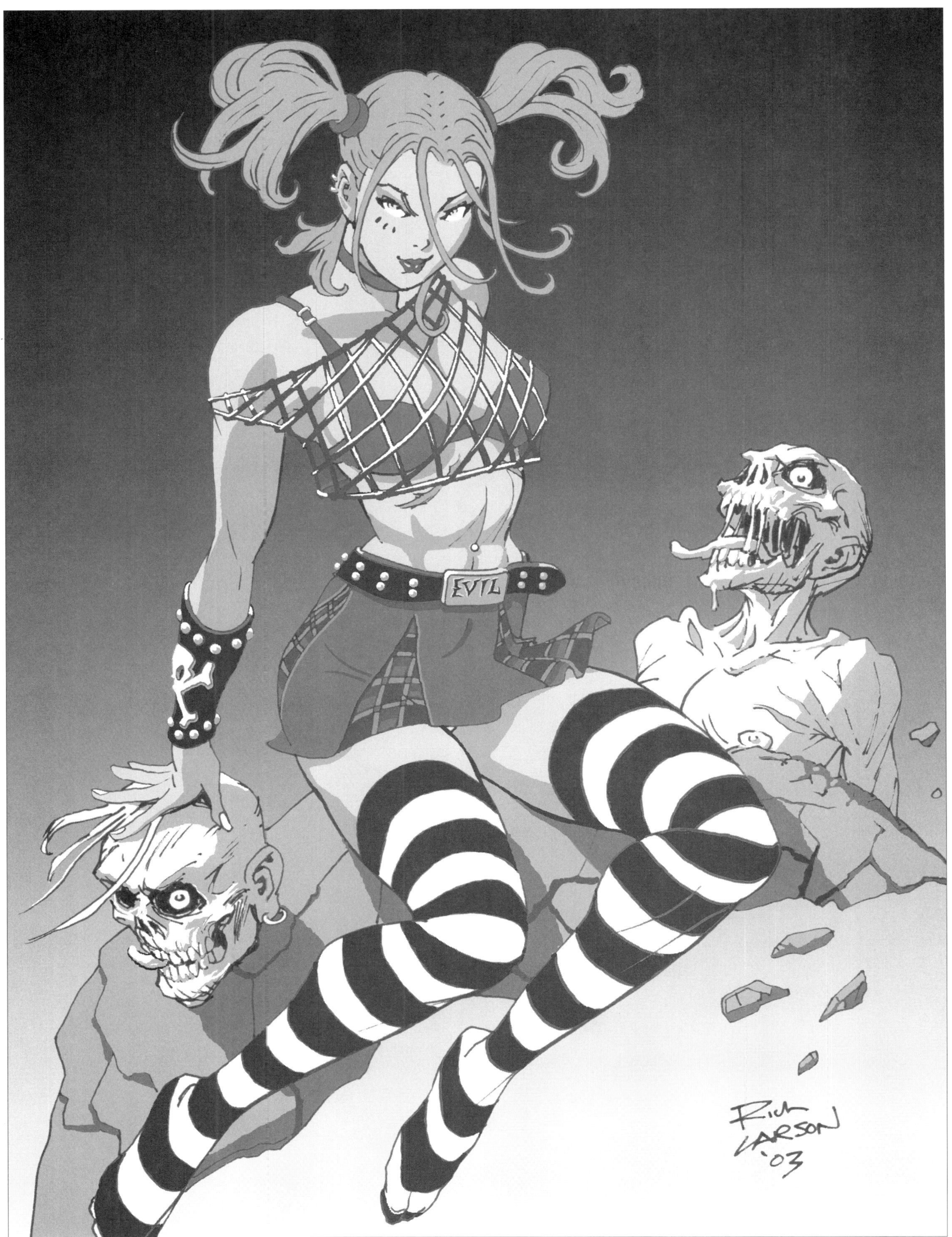

EVIL GIRL

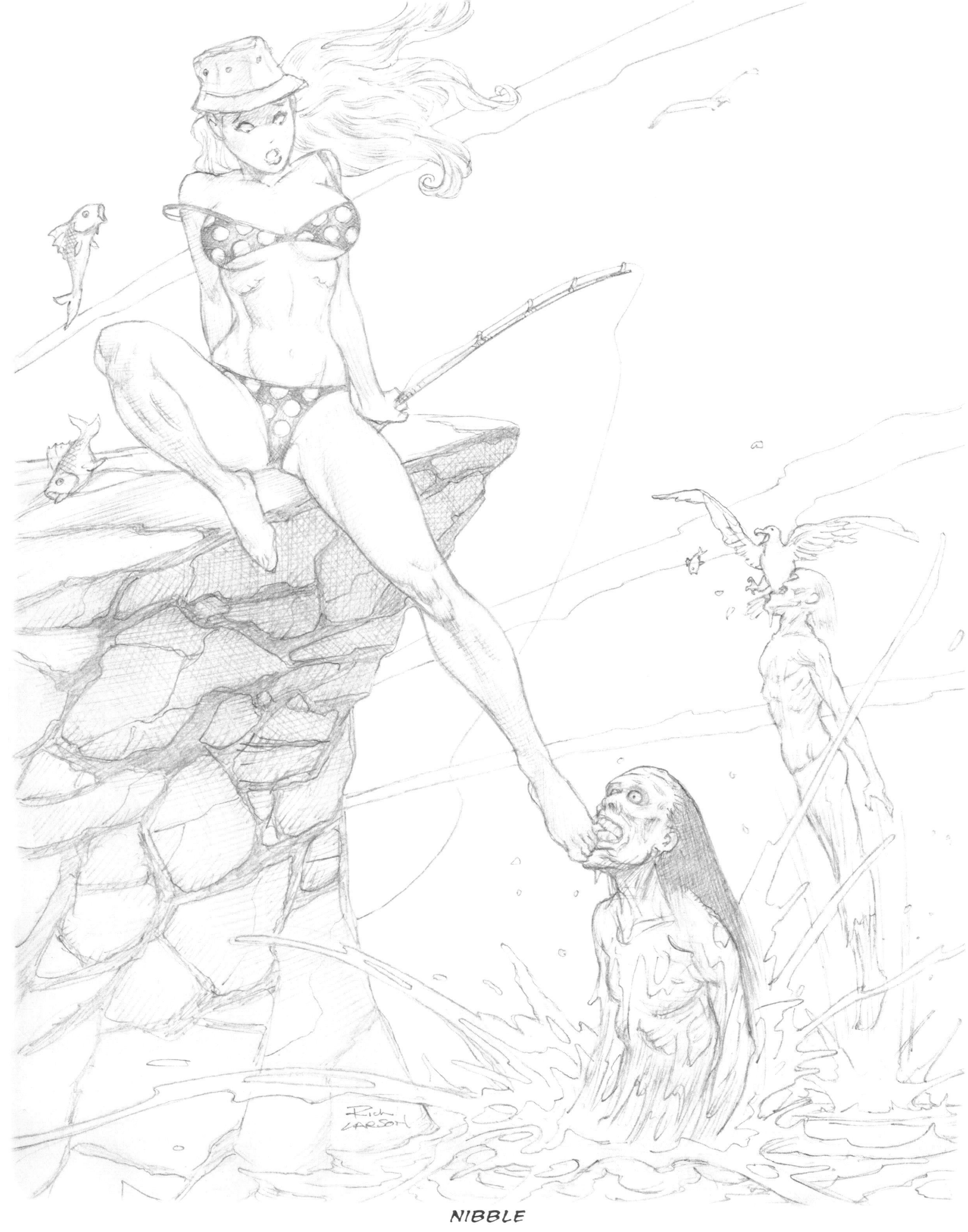

NIBBLE

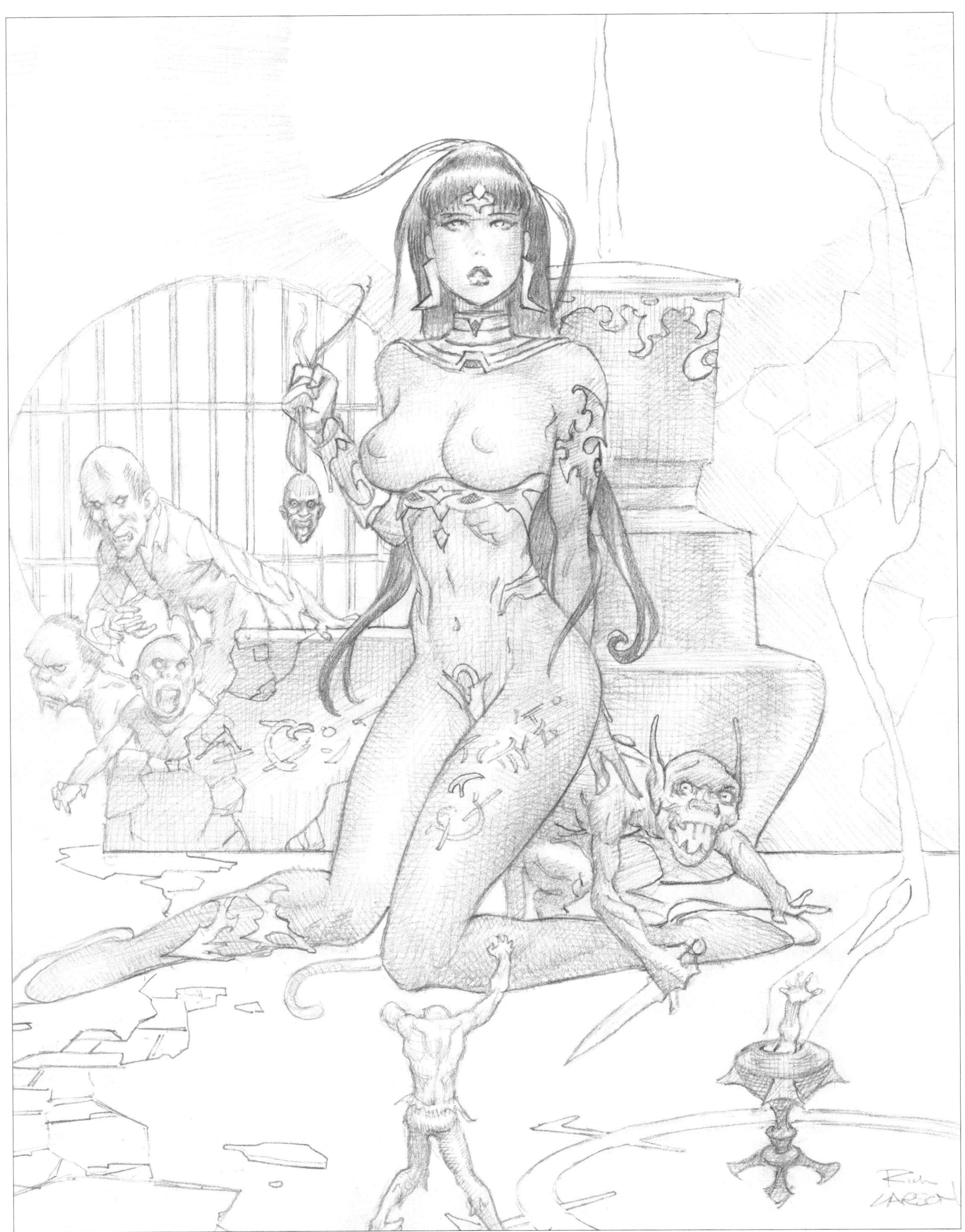

WHO'S NEXT

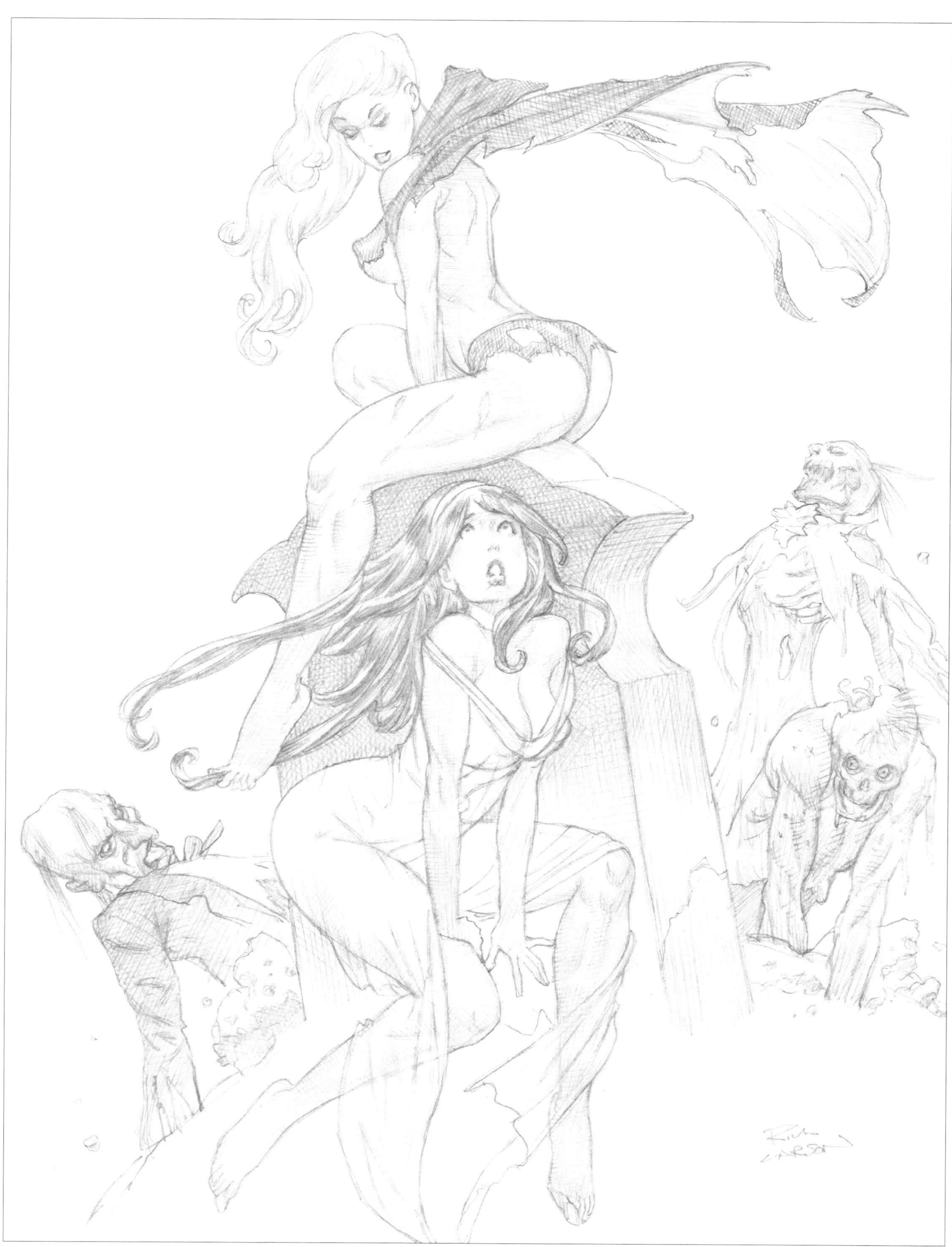

DISINTERRED BYSTANDERS

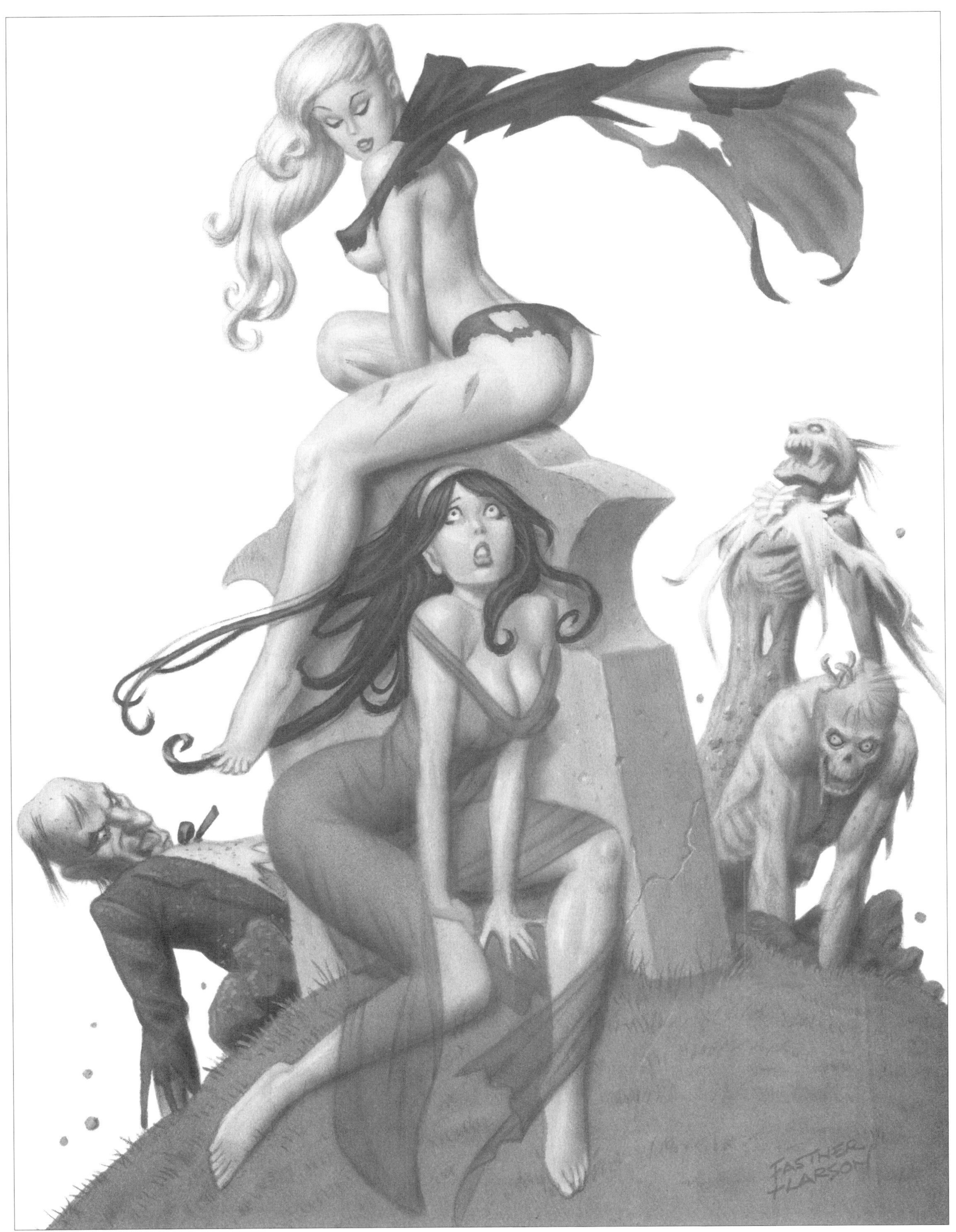

DISINTERRED BYSTANDERS PAINTING

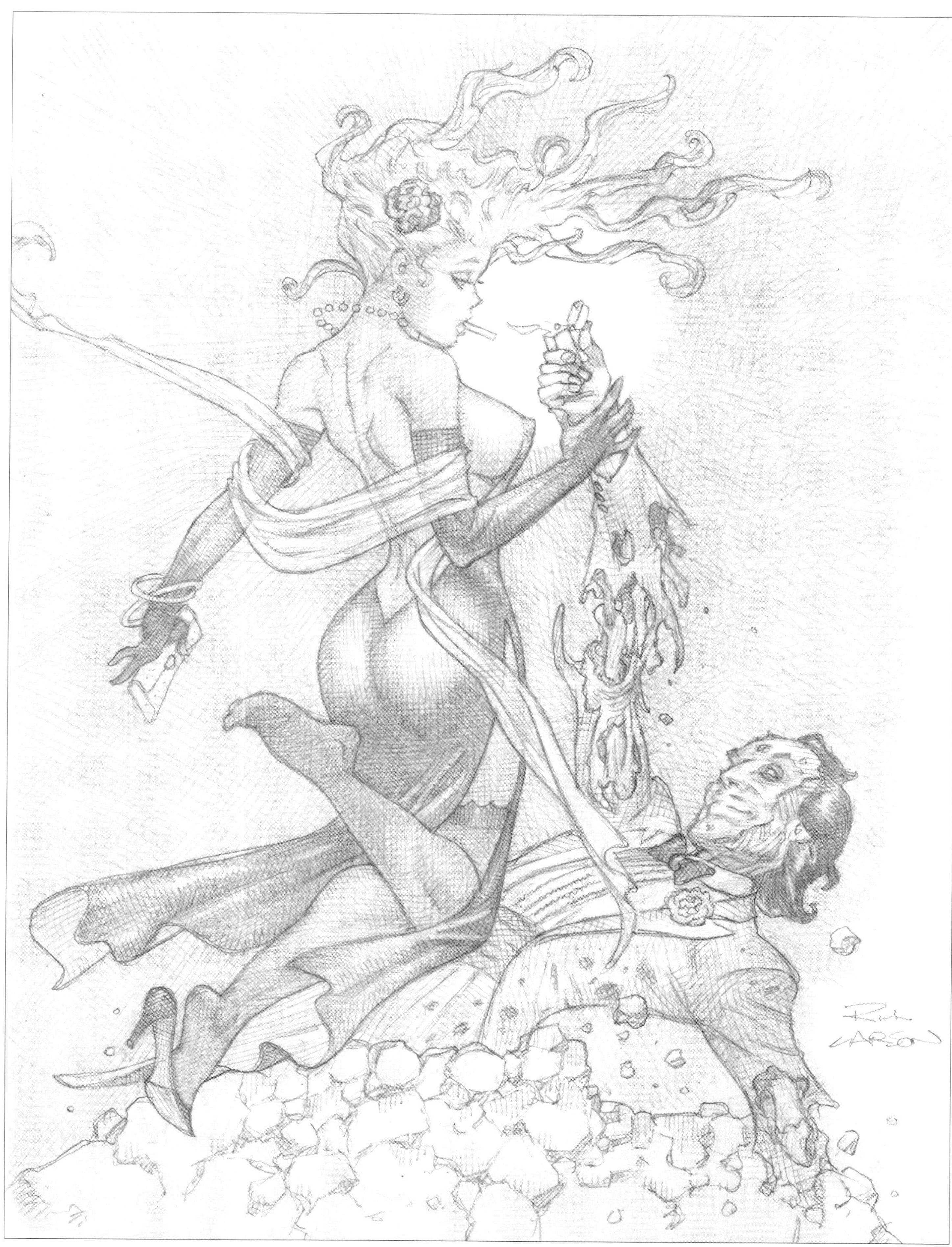

ALLOW ME

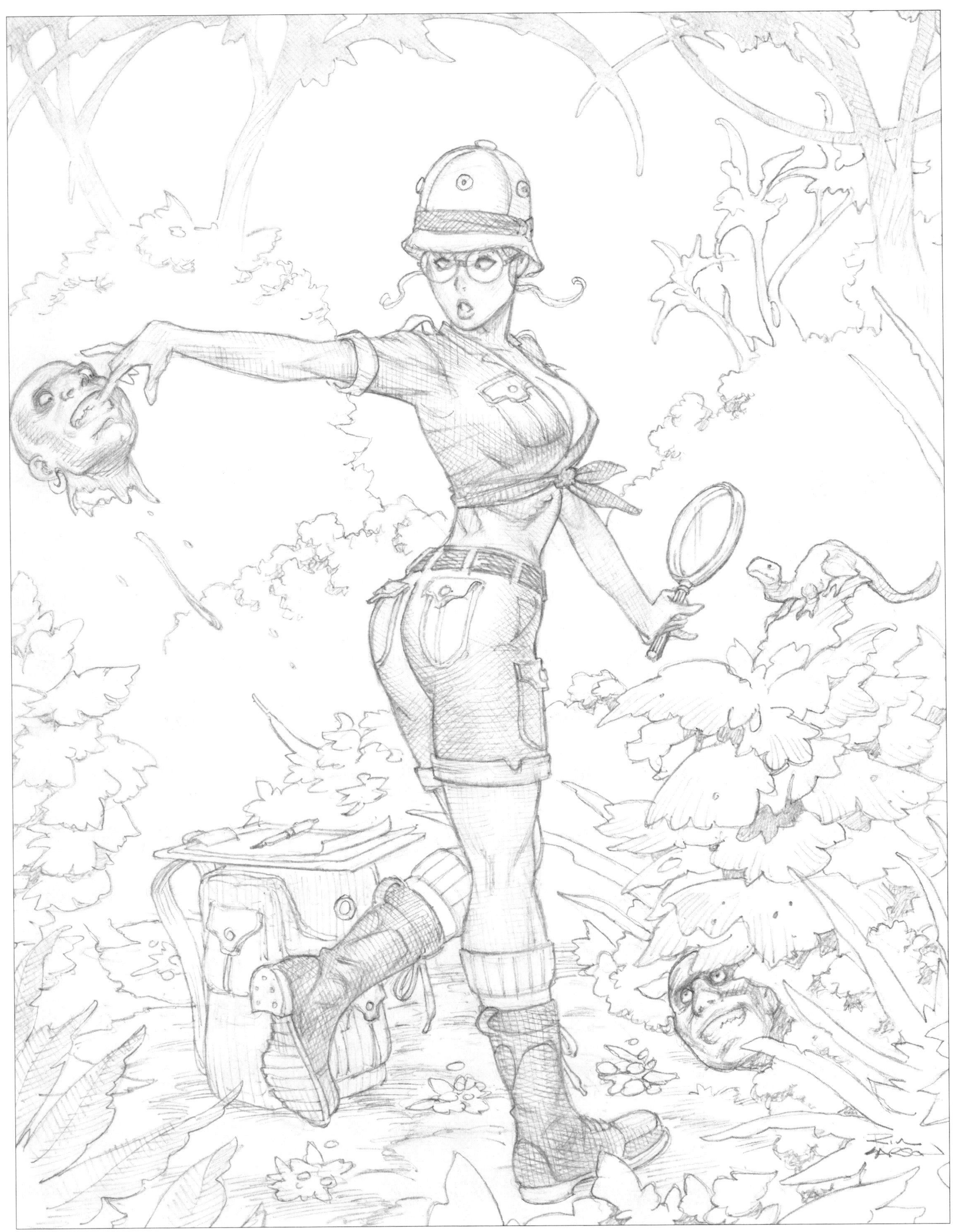

UNCHARTERED TERRITORY

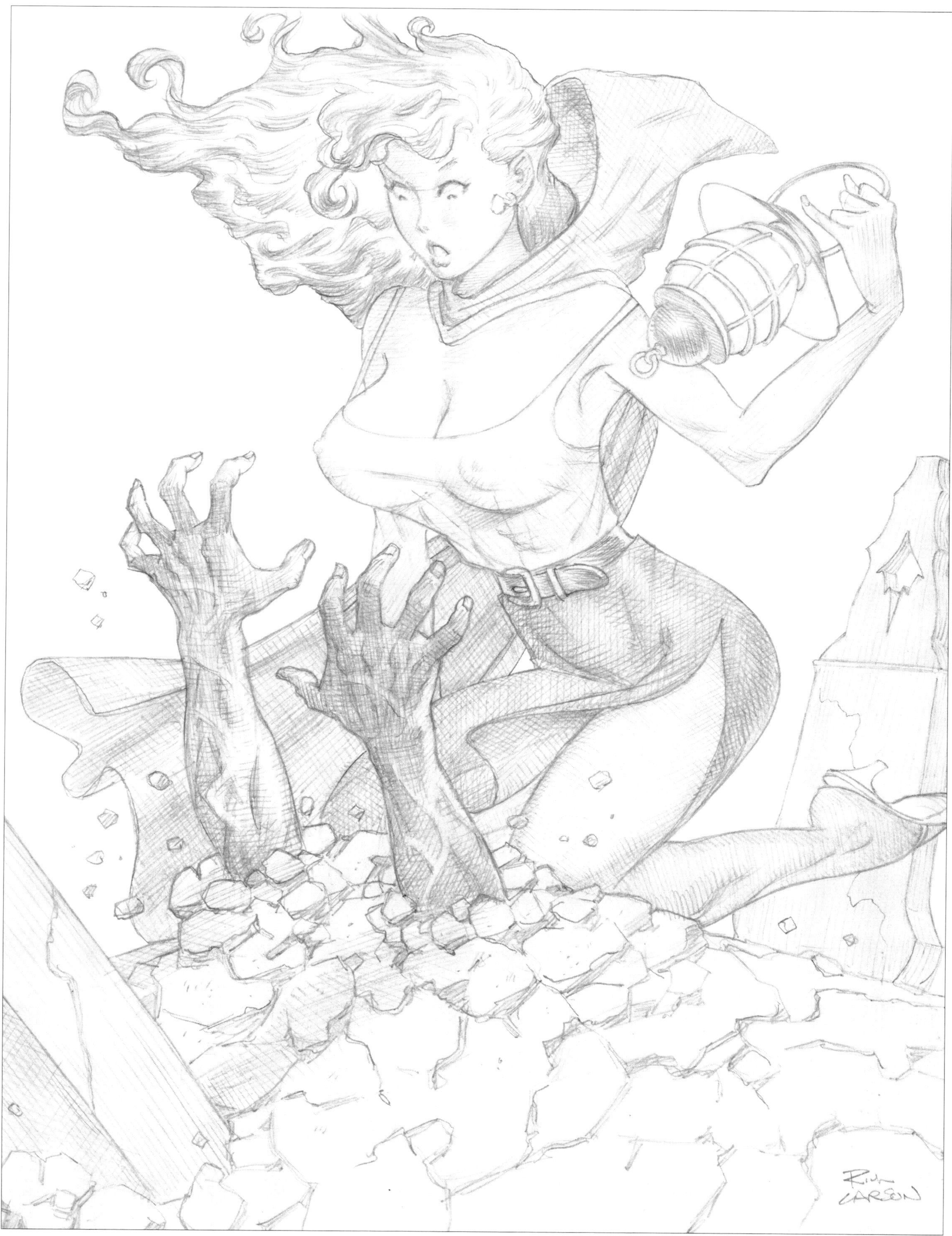

GRABBER

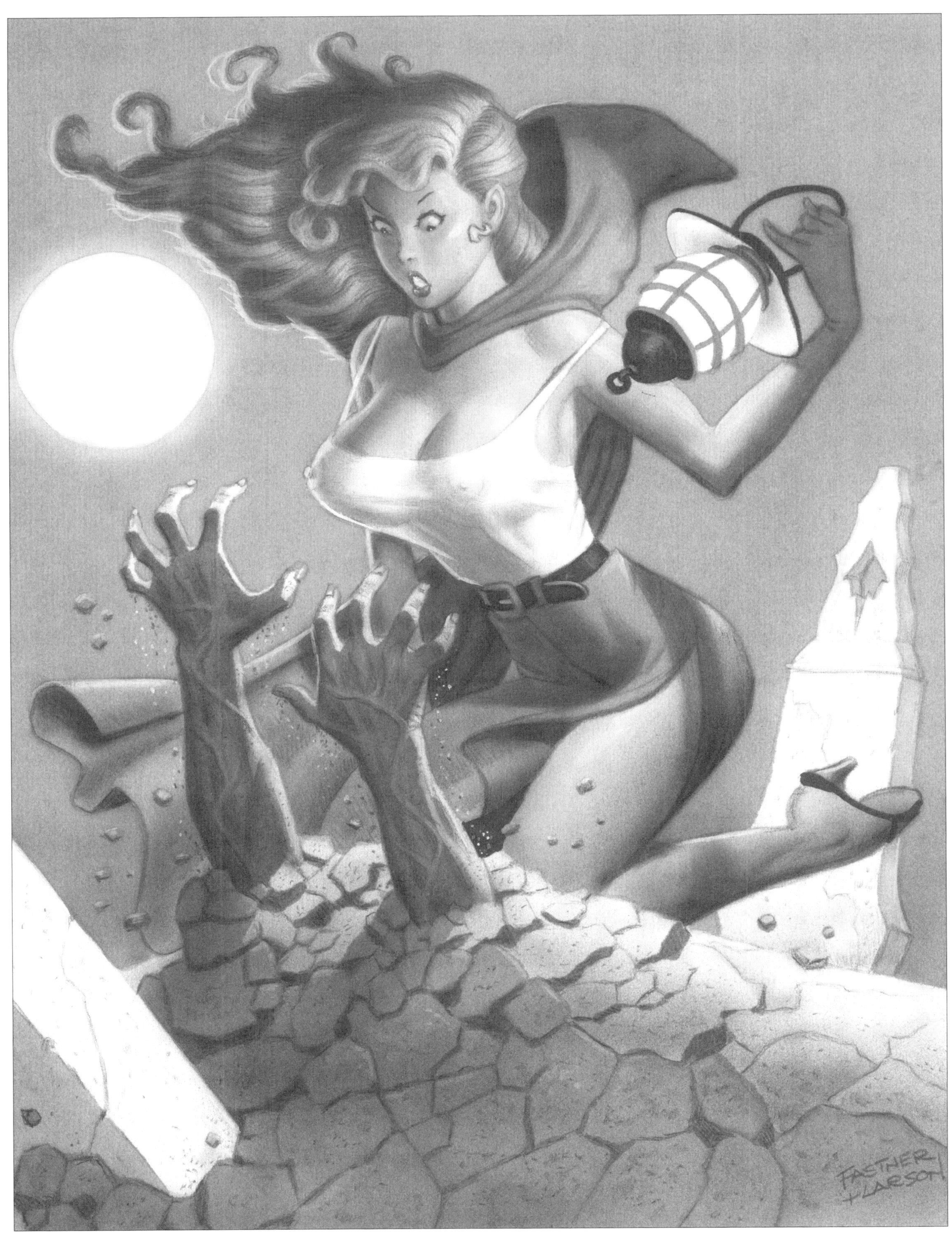

GRABBER PAINTING

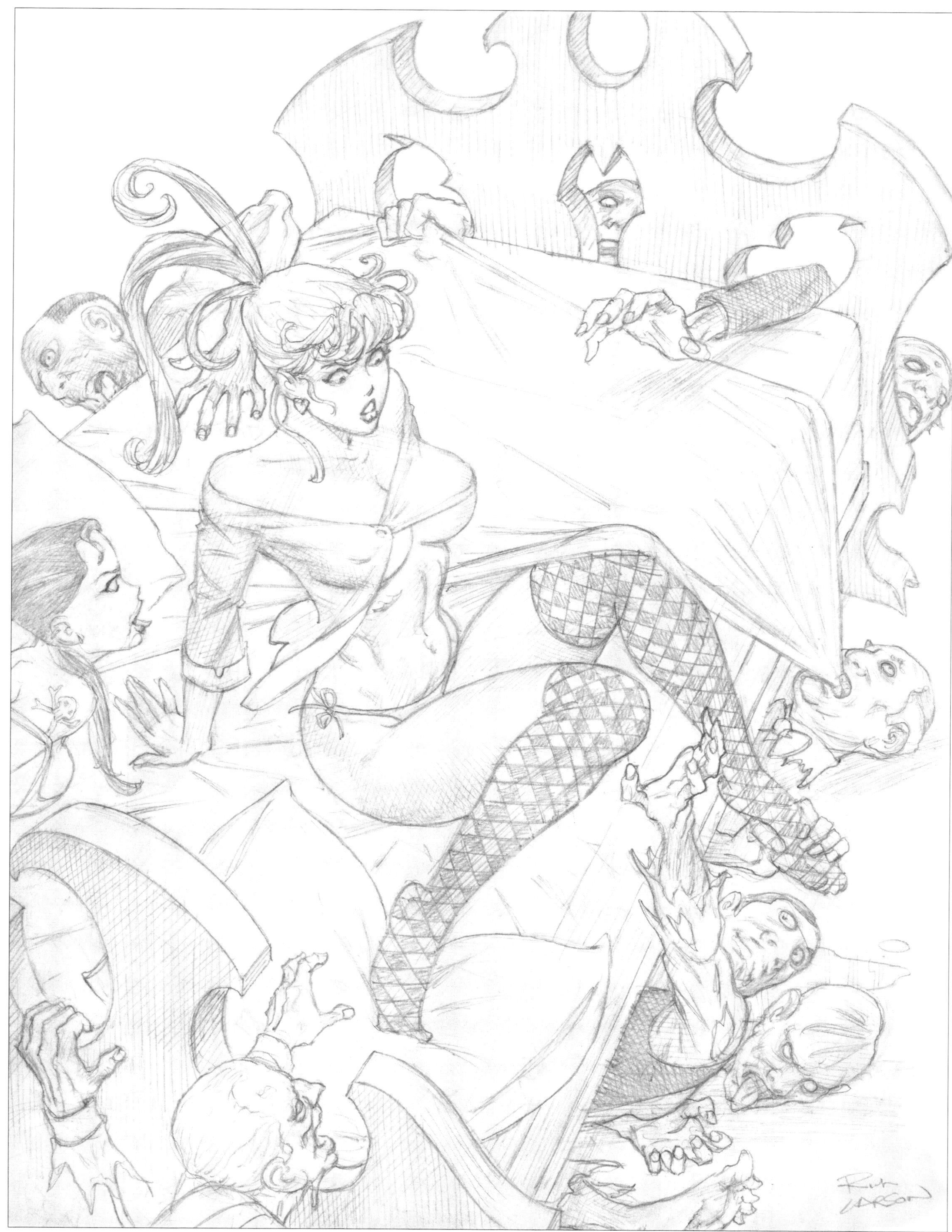

SLEEP OVER

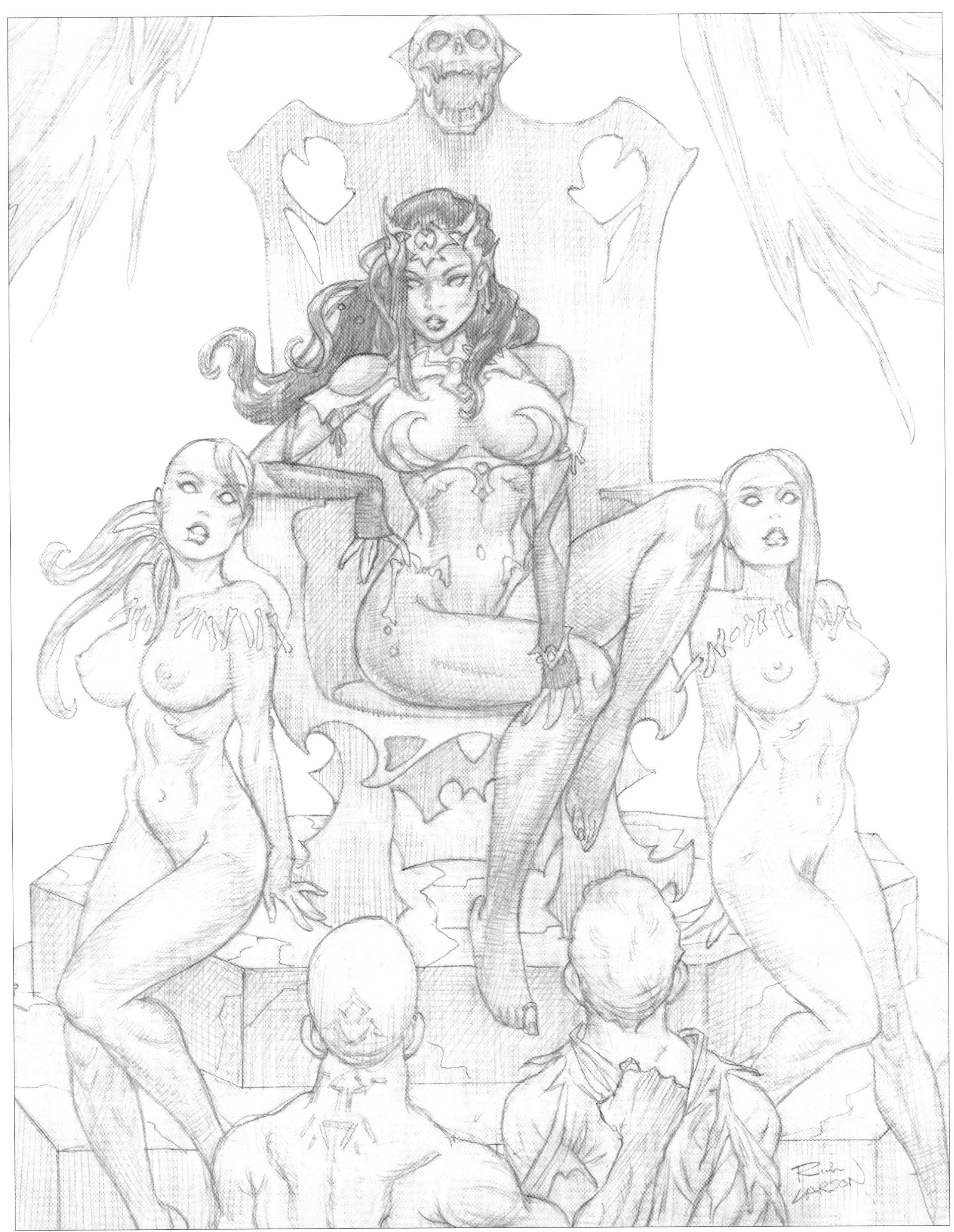

QUEEN OF THE DEAD

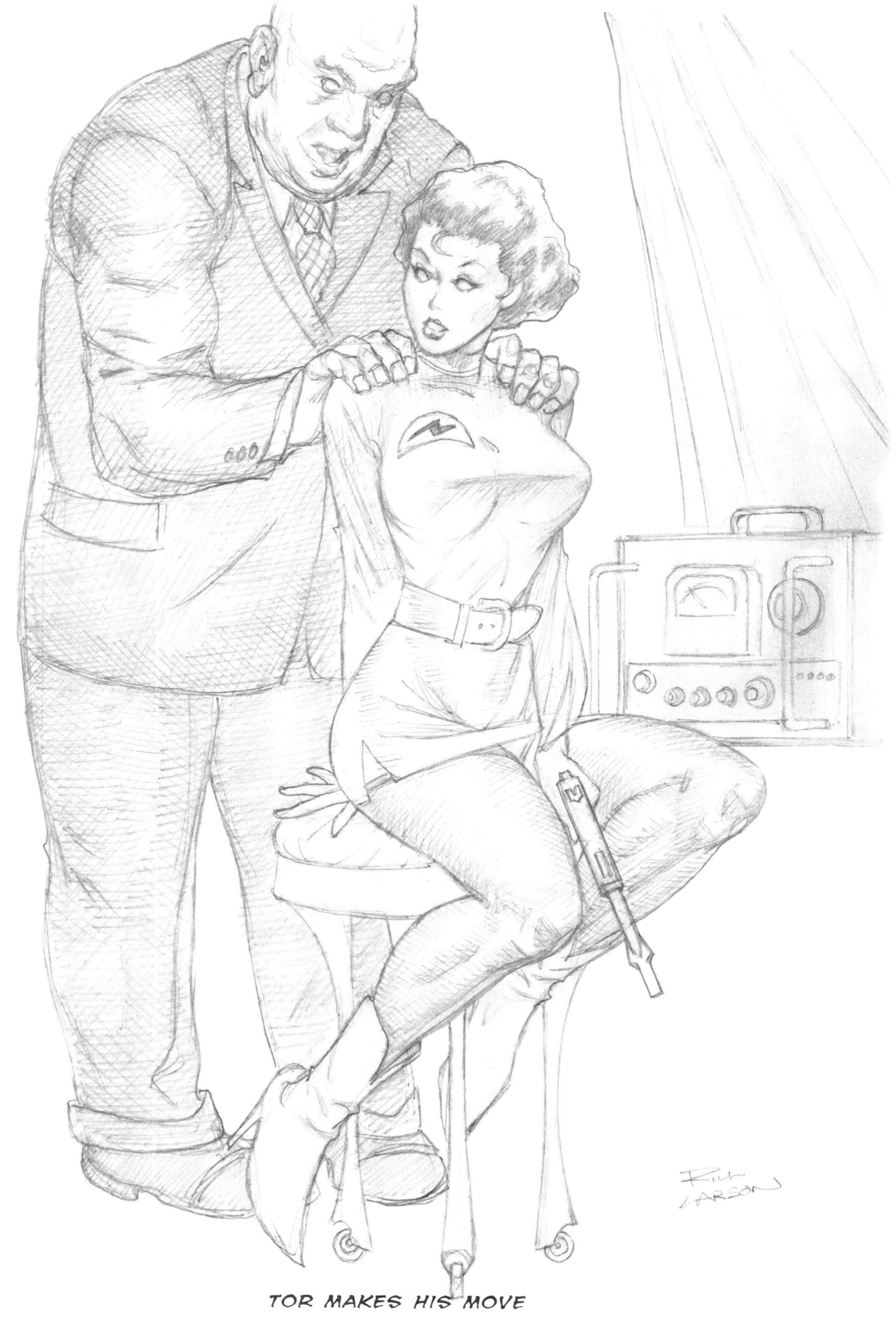

TOR MAKES HIS MOVE

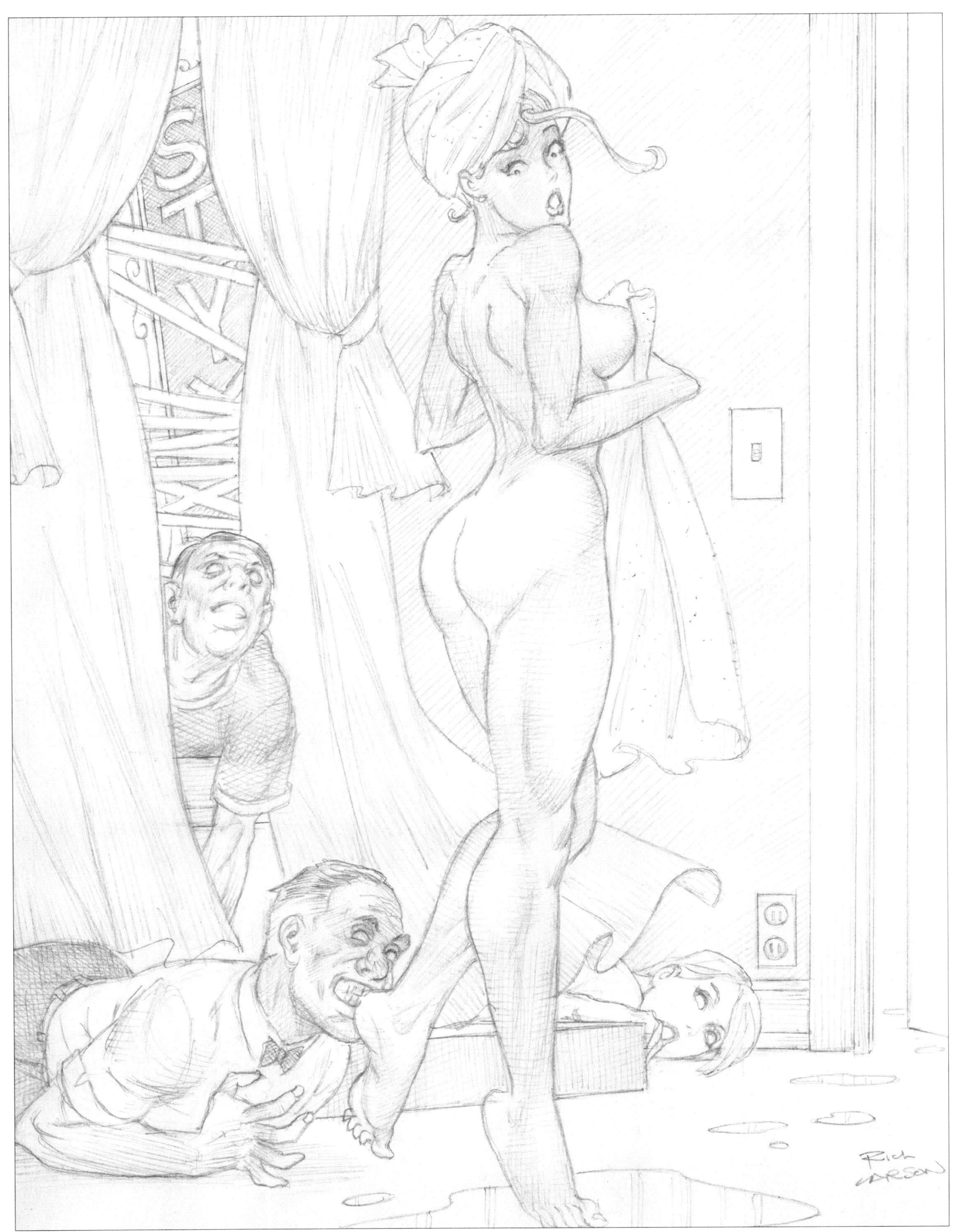

MOTEL HELL

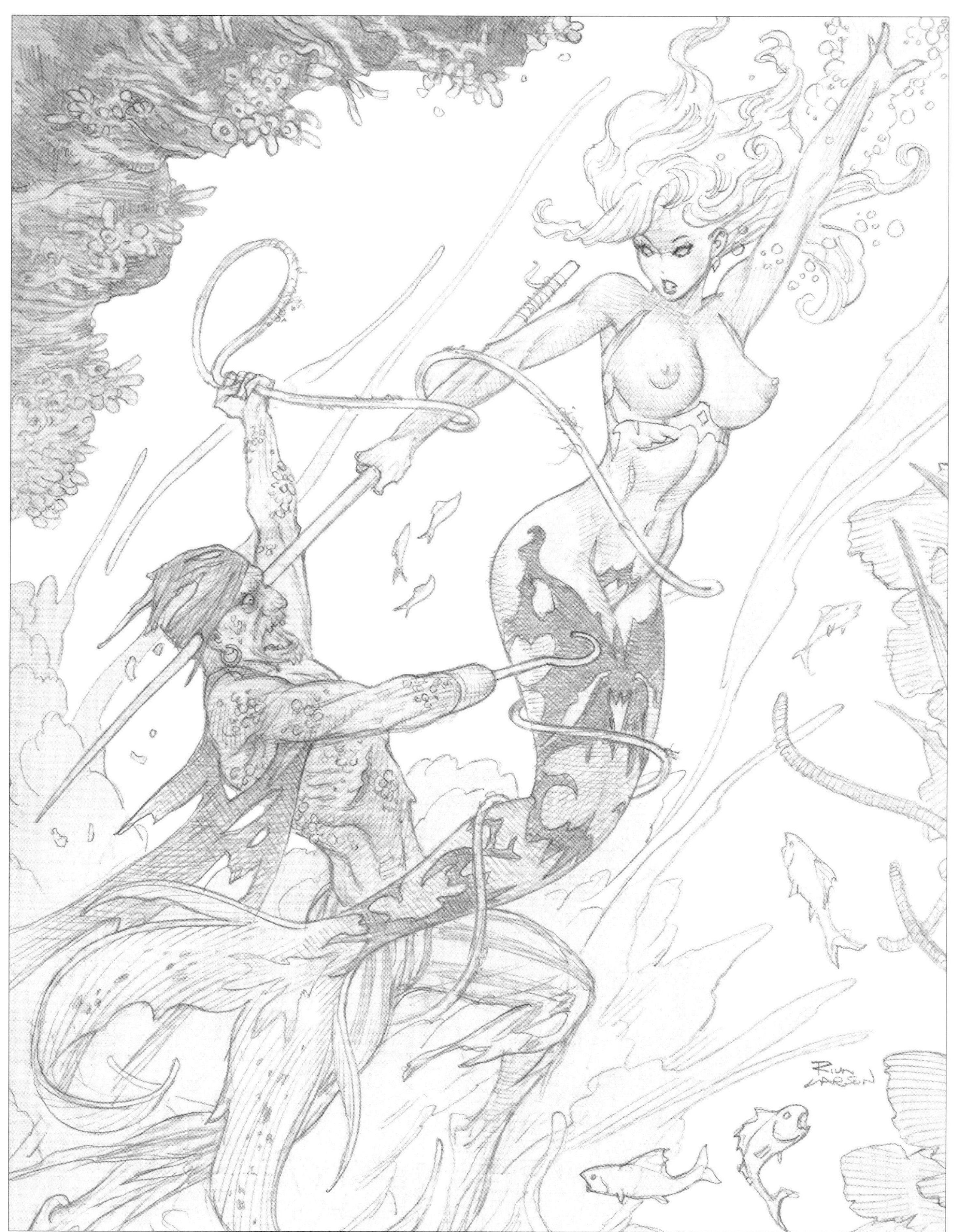

OFF THE HOOK

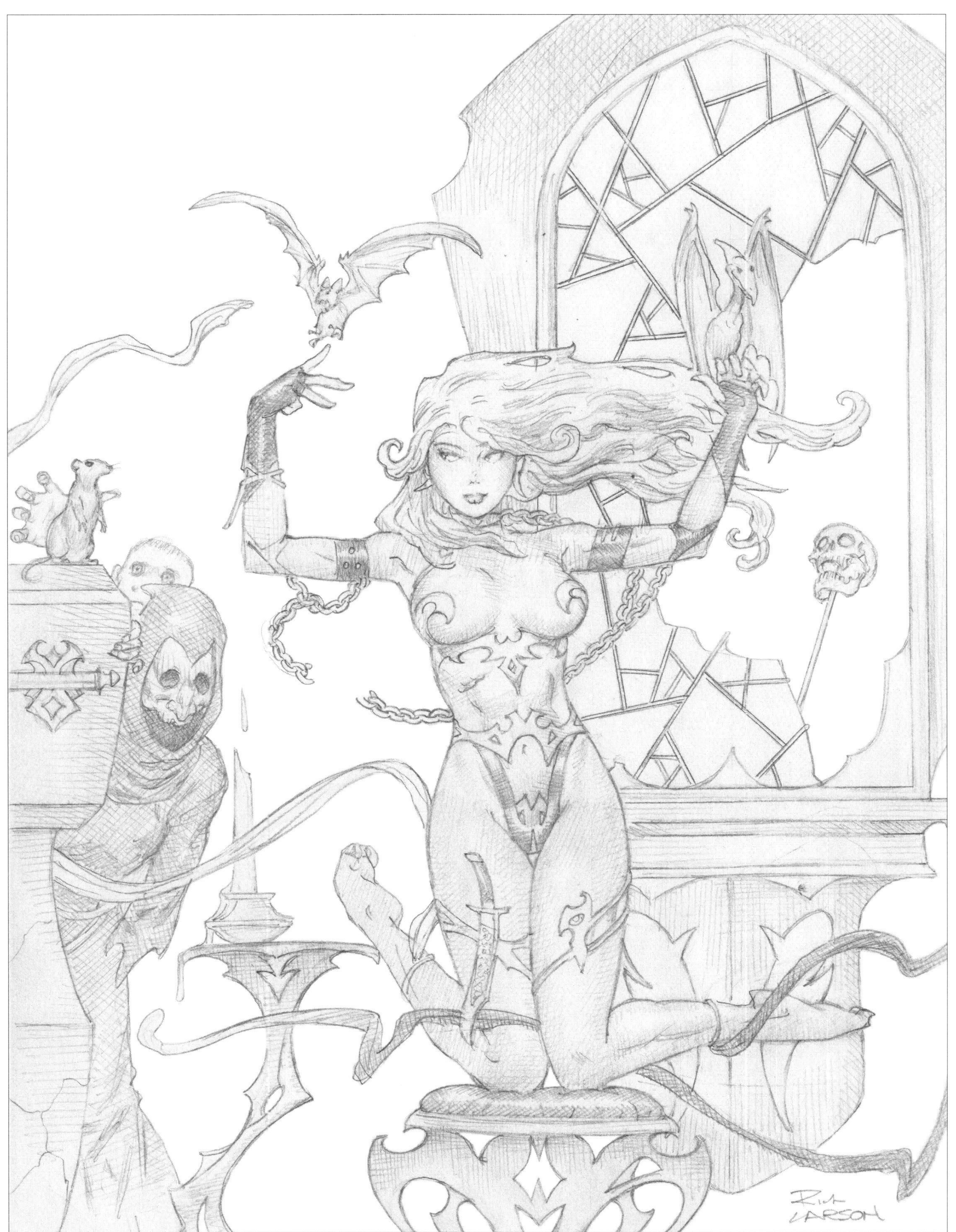

WATCHERS

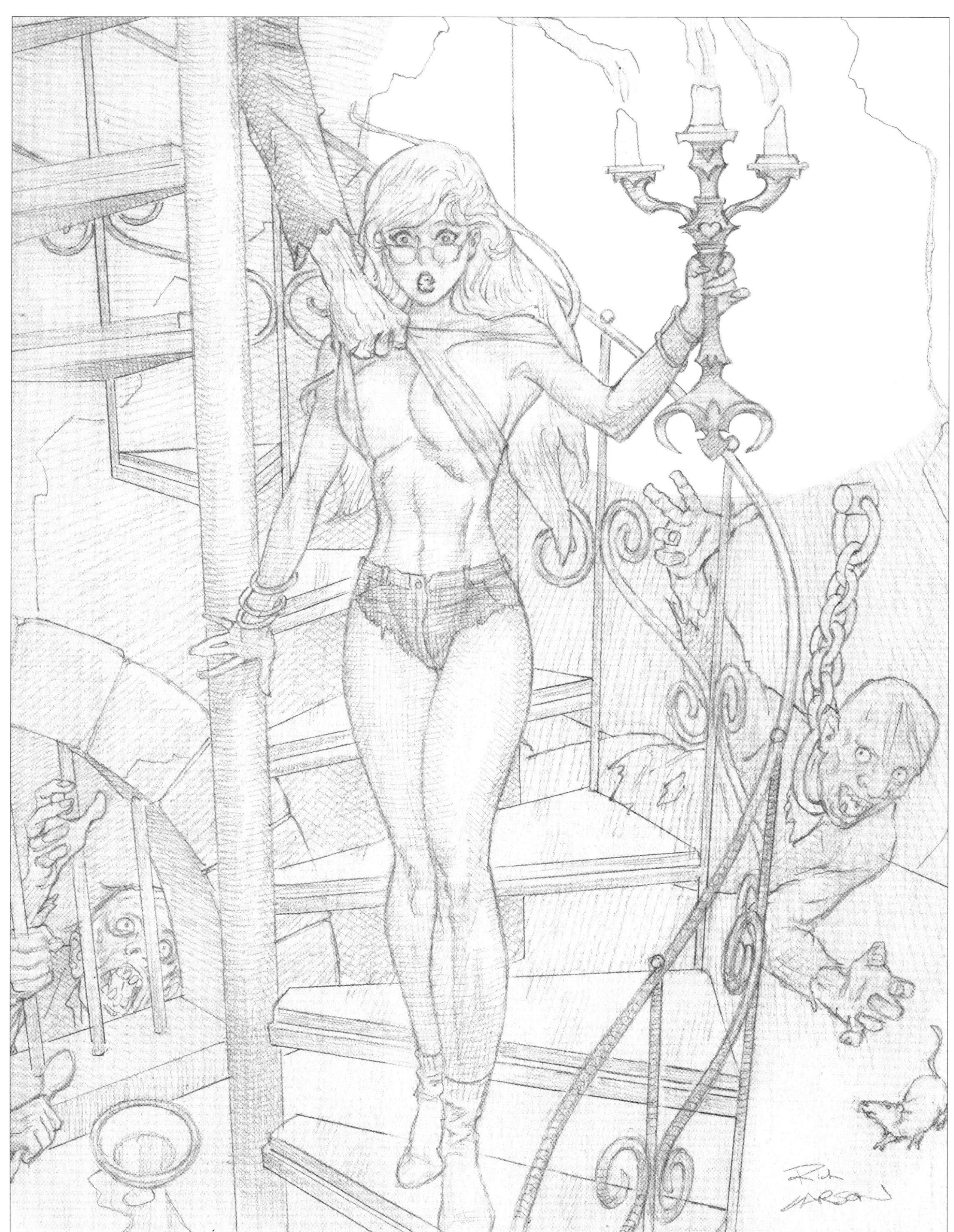

BOYFRIEND'S BASEMENT

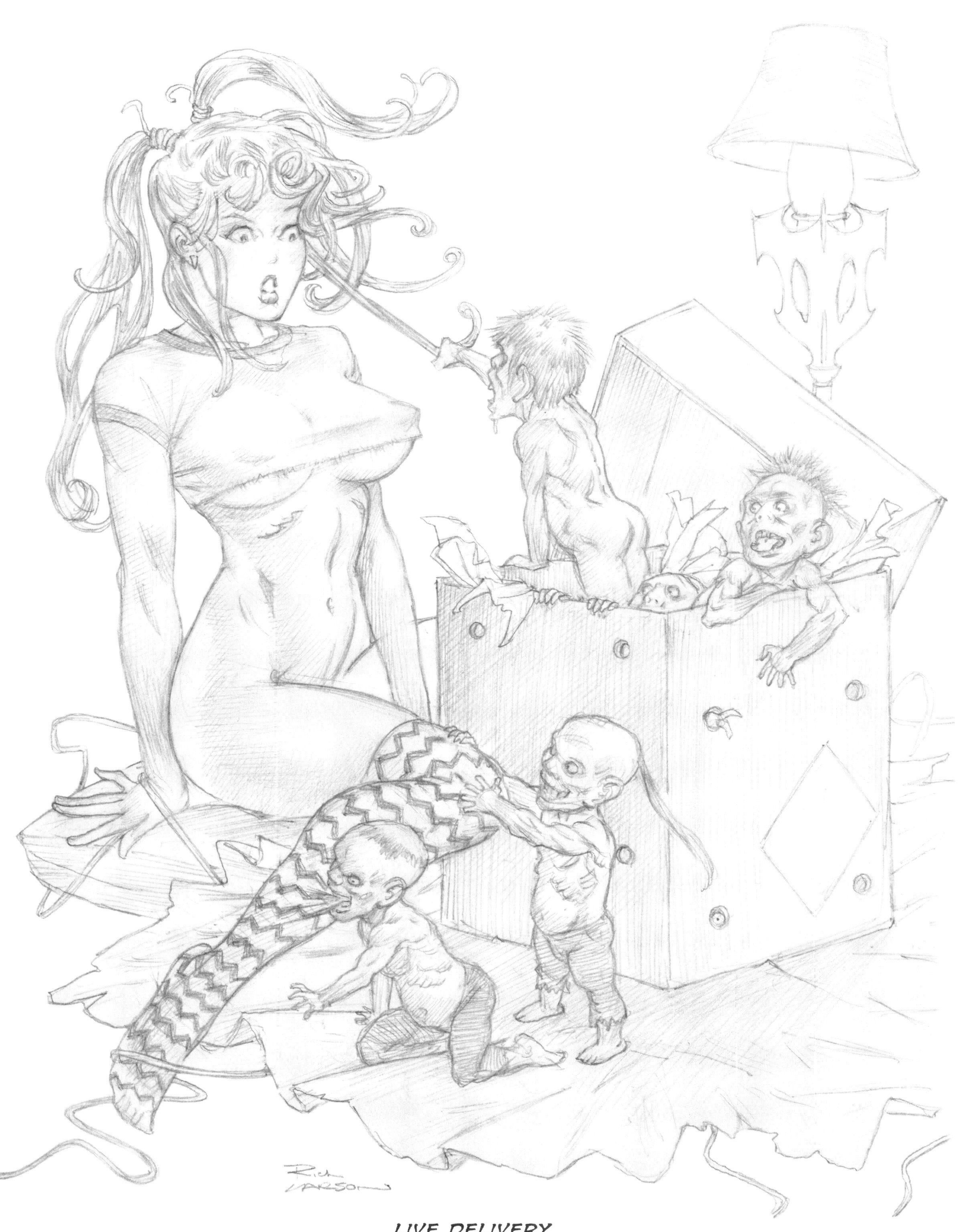

LIVE DELIVERY

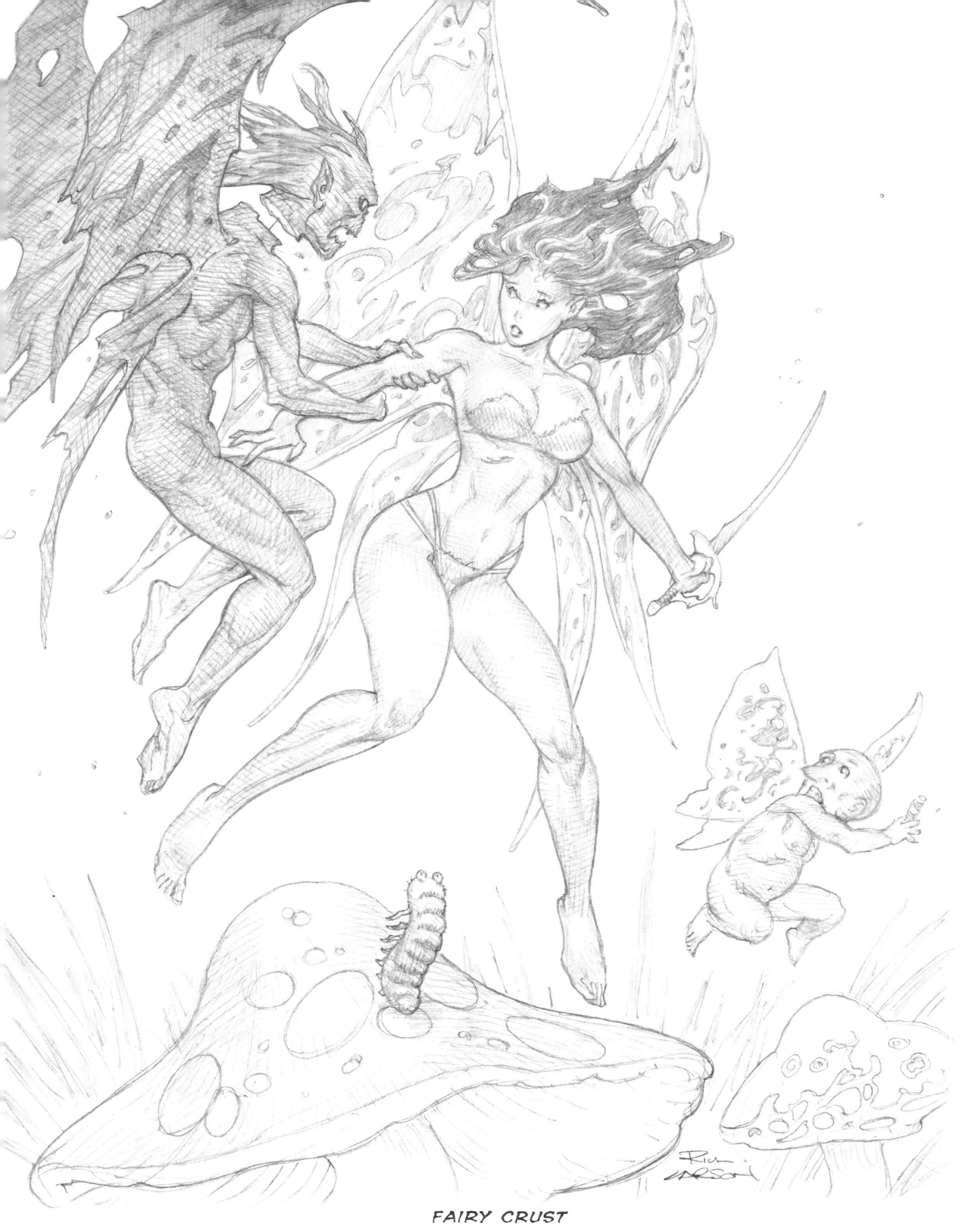

FAIRY CRUST

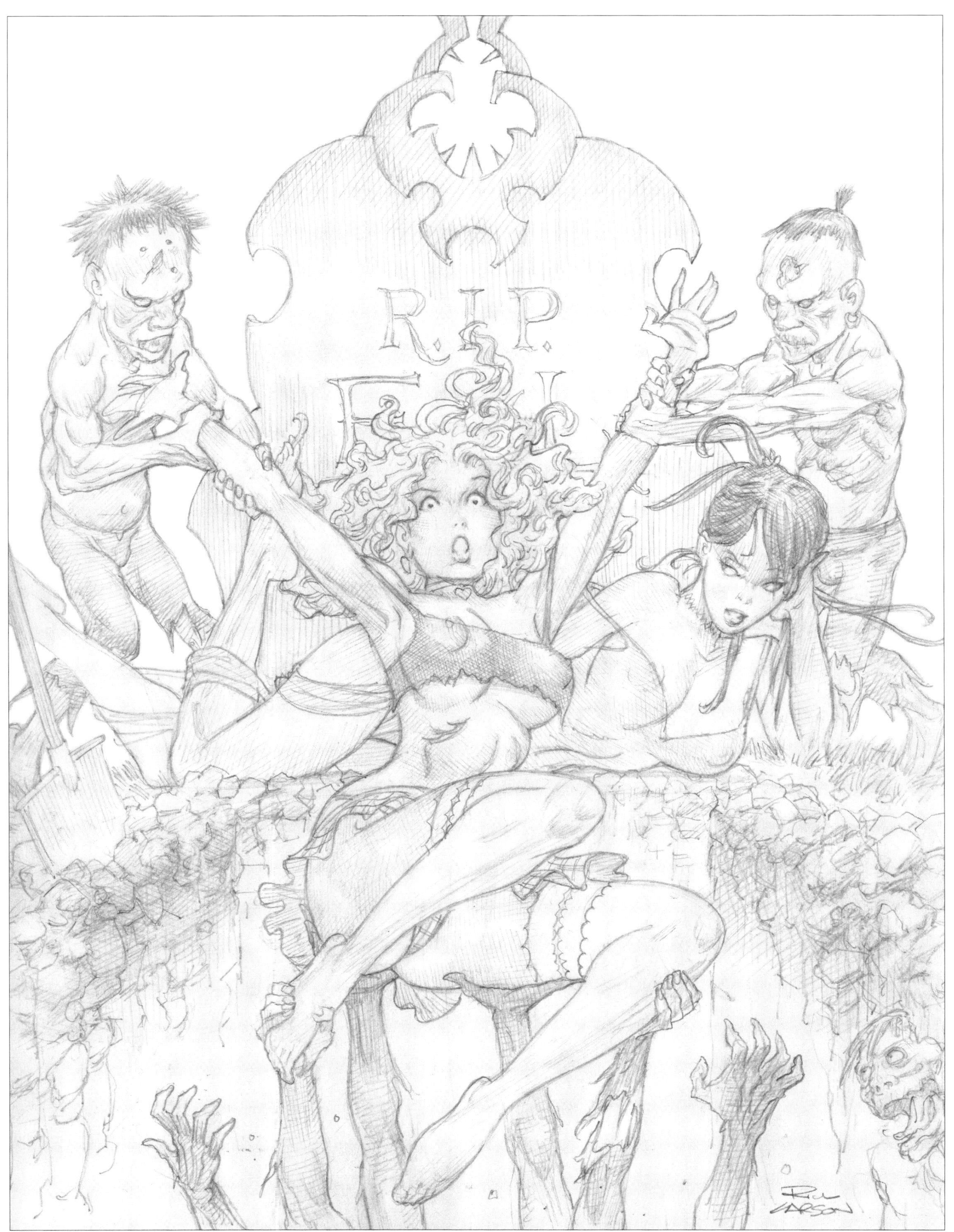

TEAMWORK

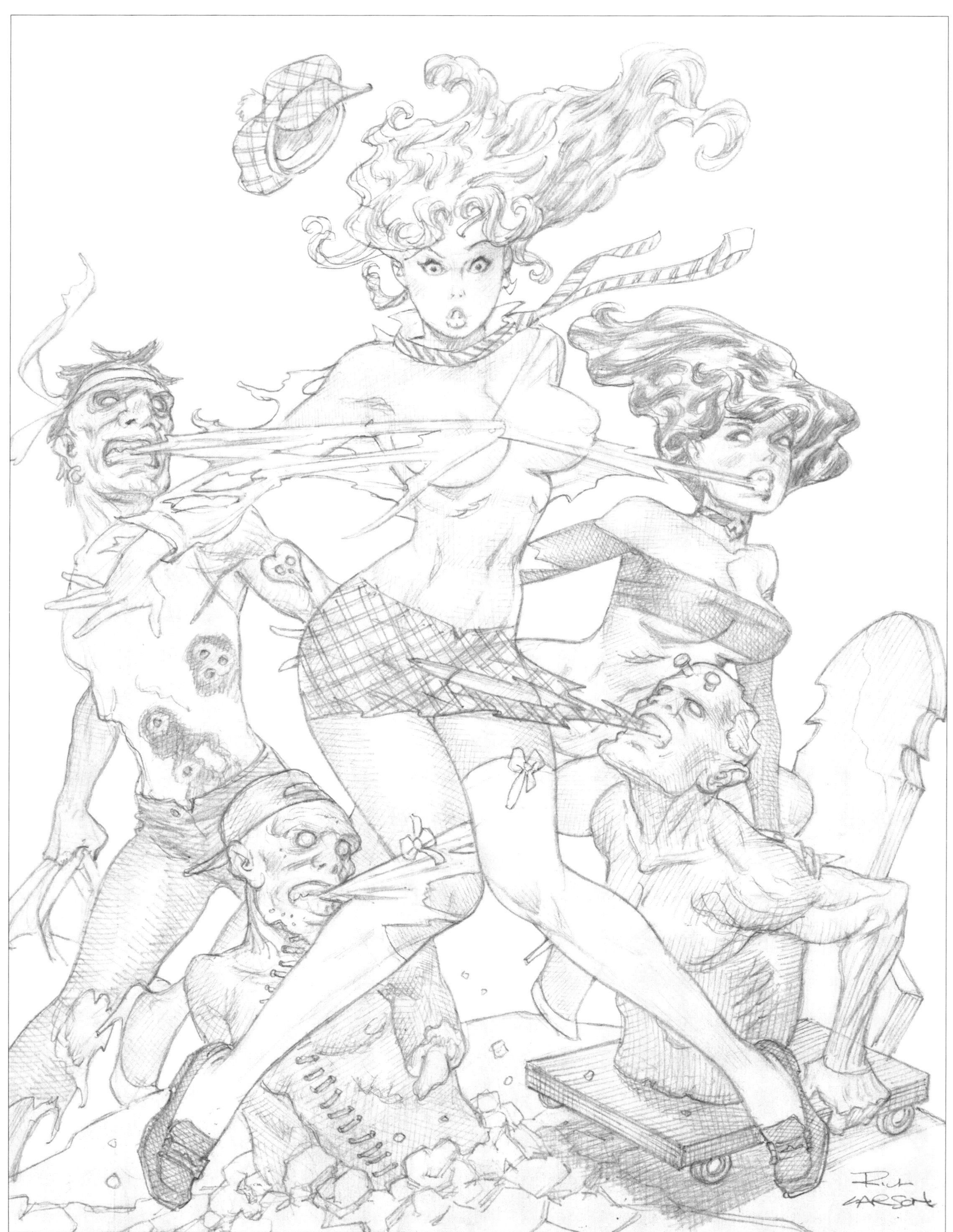

TEETH DECAY

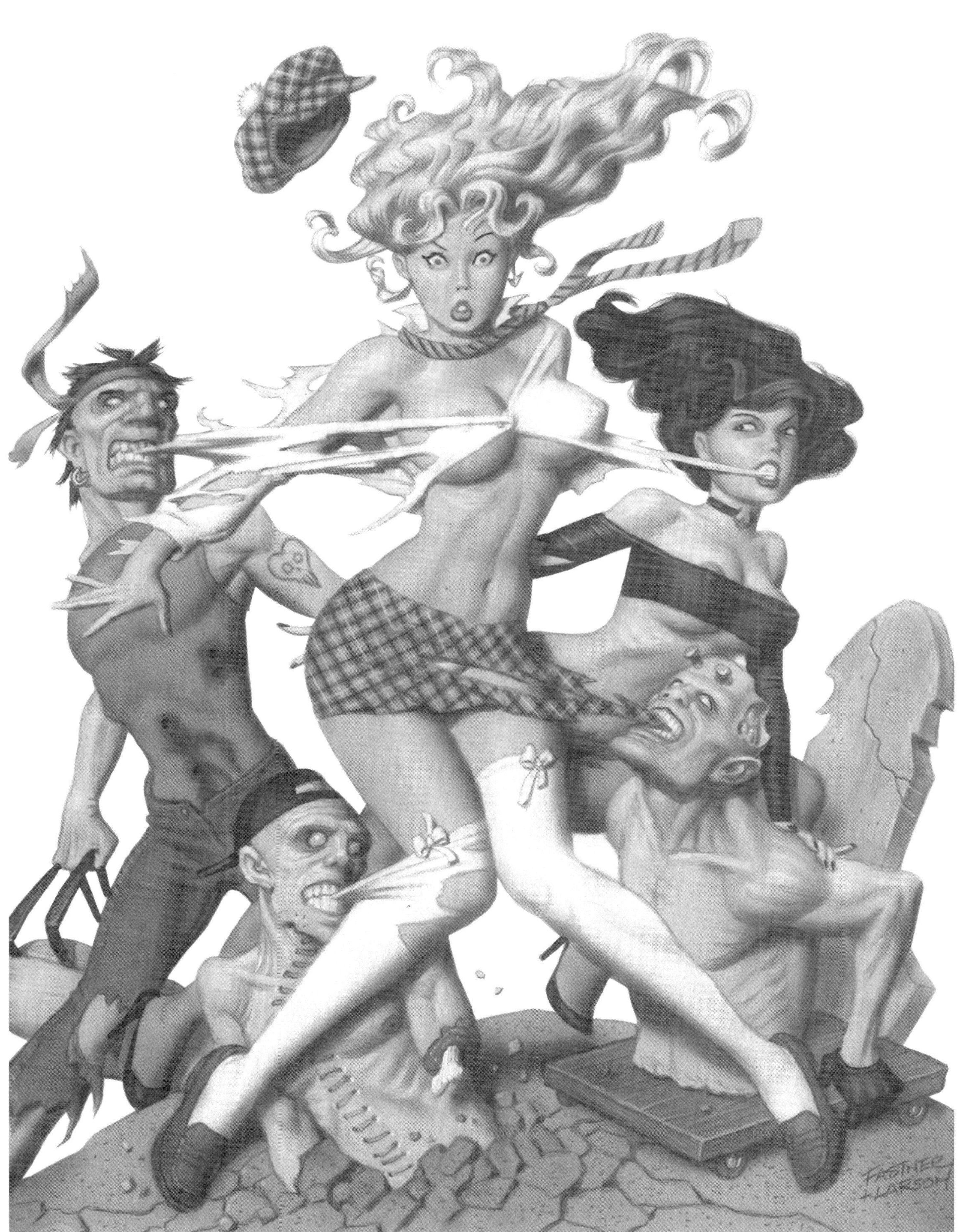

TEETH DECAY PAINTING

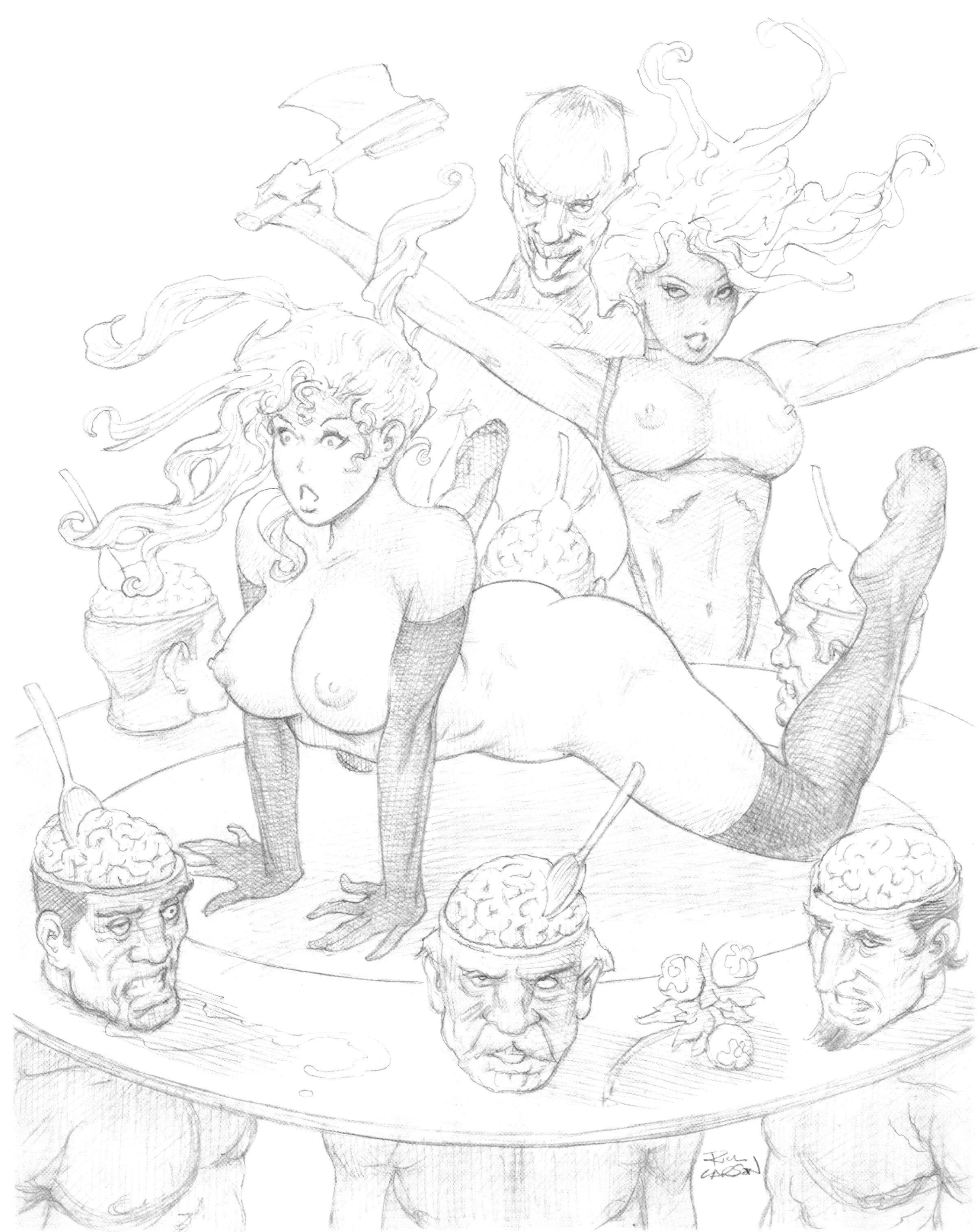

DIG IN

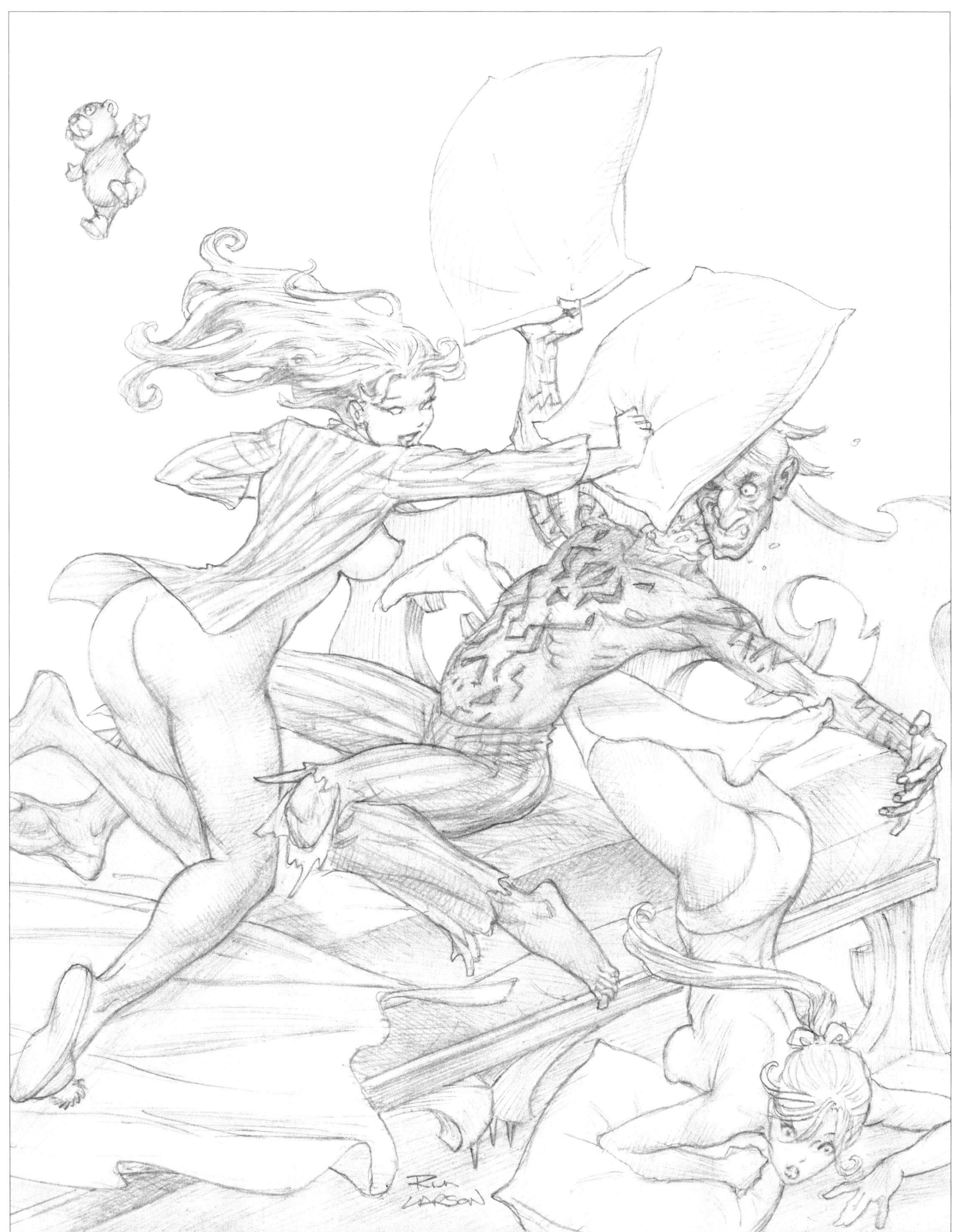

PILLOW FIGHT

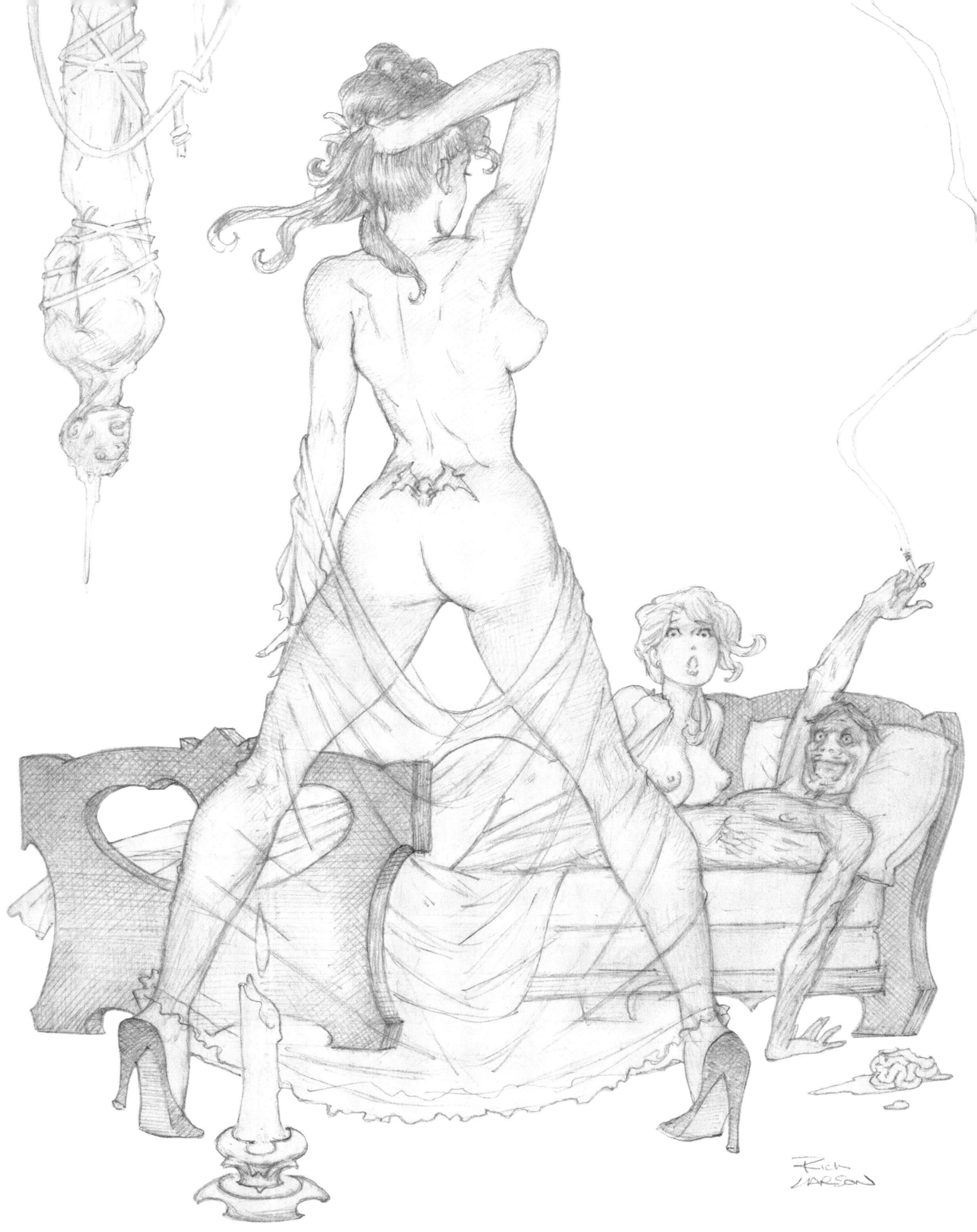

MR. POPULARITY